Small Trees

Peter McHoy

hamlyn

First published in
Great Britain in 2002
by Hamlyn, a division of
Octopus Publishing Group Ltd
2–4 Heron Quays,
London E14 4JP

ISBN 0 600 60512 4

A CIP catalogue record for this book
is available from the British Library

Printed and bound in China

10 9 8 7 6 5 4 3 2 1

This book was previously published
as *Choosing Small Trees*

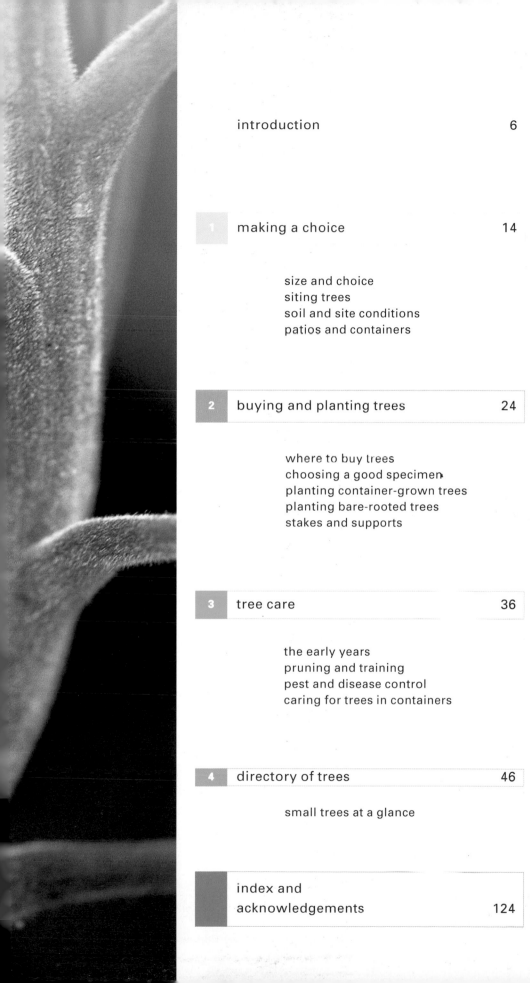

INTRODUCTION

Small gardens need trees just as much as larger plots: the **right tree** can actually make a garden look bigger by encouraging you to look upwards to the vertical space above, and they can also mask the confines of the plot.

A small tree is a **better addition** to a small garden than a large shrub. The single trunk of a tree allows more scope for underplanting than a thicket of shrub stems, and there is less need to curb the spread along the ground.

We hope you'll be inspired by this book to plant plenty of trees if your garden lacks that vital vertical element at the moment. If you already have these important backbone plants in your garden, you'll find plenty of **hints and tips** in the following pages to make the most of them.

Trees vary in **size and shape** depending on the species, but this can be manipulated by the way they are grown. While most trees have a natural shape, which is either spreading, upright or weeping, many can be trained into forms that take up less space. For example, a standard tree has a clear trunk to a height of about 1.8m (6ft) before the branches form a head at the top. A half-standard, on the other hand, has a clear trunk of about 1m (3ft) before the branches form a head.

In time, you will have the **satisfaction** of watching your chosen trees grow and mature and make their lasting contribution to the beauty of your garden.

the role of garden trees

Trees have such a physical presence that one or more trees, carefully positioned, could make the main contribution to the look and atmosphere of your garden.

Below are some examples of the role trees can play in small gardens. Remember that in any given situation a tree can perform more than one function – both screening an eyesore and providing shade, for example.

- focal points
- specimen plants
- a backbone for mixed borders
- screens
- wildlife havens

FOCAL POINTS

One of the 'tricks' when designing a small garden is to make it appear bigger than it really is by drawing the viewer's eye to certain areas. This is done by creating an illusion of a long view, using a path, low hedging or steps with something at the end for the eye to settle on. The focal point at the end of the view could be a statue, seat or fancy container, but a tree offers a natural yet long-lived focal point. In order to work as a focal point that stands out from a distance, the tree needs to be distinctive – a strong shape like an exclamation mark or a weeping standard. A bright foliage colour works well too, so consider yellow or blue-green conifers, which will stand out in contrast to the green of the rest of the garden.

SPECIMENS

Like a tree used as a focal point, a specimen has to be distinctive and capable of holding the viewer's attention on its own, but, in this case, it can be viewed from any angle and not necessarily from a distance. A single tree in a small garden may look good planted in a lawn, which may be the only space where it can develop without encroaching on neighbouring plants. For such a position, choose a subject with a feature that looks best in isolation, such as winter bark, and one that does not cast too much shade over the grass.

A BACKBONE FOR MIXED BORDERS

Trees add height and a sense of maturity to mixed borders, and together with shrubs they form a backbone. As well as looking for a contrast of shape and foliage from among the chosen woody plants, their size should be in scale with the depth of the border. Aim to include both deciduous and evergreen trees; two-thirds deciduous to one-third evergreen works well. Evergreens contribute winter interest and make a good foil for flowers,

Left: Golden conifers are especially useful during the winter months but contribute to the summer scene, too. This one harmonizes with the *Catalpa bignonioides* 'Aurea' behind.

whereas deciduous trees let enough light through in spring to allow for carpets of spring-flowering bulbs.

Other subjects that work well in mixed borders are those that cast only a light shade and those with more than one feature of interest (see planning for year-round interest, overleaf). Whenevear possible, choose and position the trees and main shrubs first, then fill in the gaps with annuals and perennials.

SCREENS

Small gardens often provide little privacy from neighbours, and eyesores such as garden sheds or fuel tanks are all too obvious. Rather than simply 'stick' a tree directly in front of the problem, experiment with placing a smaller specimen part-way between you and the object to be screened. You can either do this *in situ* by getting a friend to hold canes of various sizes at different positions in the garden or by making a simple scale model of the garden with a viewing frame and using models of trees of different shapes and sizes.

WILDLIFE HAVENS

Being longer lived and bigger, trees support a much wider range of wildlife than, say, the same area of garden given over to bedding plants or perennials. Birds and countless insects can use them as a refuge. Native trees are often considered to be preferable by purists, who say that they provide a better habitat, and of these the ones most suitable for the smaller garden include the silver birch (*Betula pendula*, see page 61) and holly (*Ilex aquifolium*, see page 80) but any tree with blossom and fruits will attract insects and birds.

Right above: *Prunus × subhirtella* 'Autumnalis' produces its semi-double white flowers intermittently all winter and has the bonus of good autumn foliage colour.

Right: Many conifers have interesting textures and colours, making them useful for combination planting. Dwarf conifers are particularly useful.

planning for year-round interest

Because trees are long-term plants they offer seasonal interest in the garden for many years, so it is worth considering them first when you are planning planting schemes for year-round colour in the garden.

Apart from the shape and form of the tree (see pages 16–17), the key seasonal features that a tree could add to the garden are:

- foliage
- flowers
- berries
- attractive bark

Above: *Robinia pseudoacacia* 'Frisia' retains a fresh-looking golden colour throughout the summer months.

FOLIAGE

An evergreen will offer foliage all year round, although it will be appreciated most in winter and early spring when there is little else in leaf. Deciduous trees are in leaf from spring to autumn, and the colour might change through these seasons – some species are noted for their brilliant autumn tints. Aim for a balance of evergreen and deciduous woody subjects – too many evergreens will make for a static, sombre garden with less seasonal variety, but too many deciduous trees can leave a garden looking bare and structureless in winter.

Flowers are impressive for a short while, but a tree with attractive foliage will give a longer period of interest. Apart from the many shades of green, some species offer golden-yellow foliage (*Catalpa bignonioides* 'Aurea', for example, see page 65); red or purple foliage (such as *Fagus sylvatica* 'Purpurea Pendula', see page 79); silver or grey foliage (*Pyrus salicifolia* 'Pendula', see page 109) and variegated foliage (many varieties of English holly, *Ilex aquifolium*, see page 80). Pale colours like grey-silver, blue-green or paler greens are useful in a small garden, and trees of these

Above: *Acer palmatum* 'Osakazuki' is one of many fine Japanese maples. These trees are often shrub-like while they are young.

colours positioned at the far end of the plot will make it appear longer.

For golden-yellow foliage all through the summer *Robinia pseudoacacia* 'Frisia' (see page 113) takes some beating and has become a popular choice in many gardens.

autumn leaf colour

For late-season interest some trees offer brilliant autumn tints that almost set the sky alight, while others offer displays of fruits. Such seasonal highlights will not necessarily put on a dazzling display every year as they are weather dependent. Some years strong winds strip the leaves off the trees while they are looking their most colourful. When the weather turns harsh early, birds may strip trees of berries almost overnight. If possible, choose a tree that offers more than just berries or autumn colour.

The best autumn leaf colour is usually seen where trees are growing on poor soils, such as thin, chalky or sandy soils, but there are exceptions, such as *Cornus kousa* (see page 69), so check the details in the Directory of Trees. Even with the same species some varieties have a reputation for producing better colour than others. *Acer griseum* has reliable autumn colour. Another good one is *Malus tschonoskii* (see page 93) with leaves of yellow, orange, purple and

Below: *Prunus* × *yedoensis* 'Shidare-yoshino' (sometimes found with the name *P.* 'Yoshino Pendula') has branches that may weep to the ground.

scarlet. The stag's horn sumach (*Rhus typhina*, see page 111) has large, pinnate leaves which are brightly coloured in autumn and there may also be hairy, cone-shaped autumn fruits.

winter foliage

Conifers come into their own during the winter with their evergreen foliage in various colours and look especially effective when combined with ornamental grasses or with winter- or spring-flowering heathers for extra interest. The Irish yew (*Taxus baccata* 'Fastigiata') is grown for its easy-to-keep-neat column shape. Use it on its own as a focal point or plant in rows for a formal effect.

FLOWERS

Most trees with spectacular blooms tend to produce them either in spring or in summer. Trees like the Japanese cherries, magnolias and laburnum look stunning when they are in full flower, but they generally offer little for the rest of the year, so take this into account when you are planning year-round colour. By all means use them as seasonal highlights but combine them with colourful evergreens or plants with more than one season of interest.

Above: *Prunus incisa* is a lovely flowering cherry for spring, and the variety 'Praecox' will even bloom during the winter.

Below: *Sorbus aucuparia* is grown mainly for its super display of bright red berries. Unfortunately, birds also find these very attractive and often the trees can be stripped prematurely.

spring flowers

Catkins are an early herald of spring and these can be provided in a small garden by choosing *Salix caprea* 'Kilmarnock' (see page 115), a small, umbrella-like tree with silvery catkins and gold anthers. Young foliage on many deciduous trees can also provide fresh, bright colour as the leaves unfold.

There are a great many spring-flowering trees to choose from, so remember to be selective: a small garden will probably accommodate no more than two or three. The Japanese cherry trees are well known for their lovely spring blossom. *Prunus* 'Amanogawa' (see page 95) has fragrant, semi-double, shell pink flowers, *P.* 'Kanzan' (see page 99) has deep pink buds that open to fully double, rich pink flowers, while the cascading *P.* 'Kiku-shidare-zakura' (see page 100) has pink buds and fully double, rose pink flowers.

Late spring is the time for *Amelanchier lamarckii* (see page 57) to become covered in clouds of starry white flowers. One of the earliest flowering crab apples is *Malus floribunda* (see page 89) with its deep pink buds opening to pale pink, then white flowers. Magnolias, such as *Magnolia* × *soulangeana* (see page 86) always impress with their primitive, tulip-like flowers on the leafless branches. Choose a named variety so the tree will flower when it is young.

Other possibilities include the white, pink or red flowers of *Crataegus* (hawthorn) species and hybrids; the yellow pea flowers of the pea tree (*Caragana arborescens*, see page 63) and the Judas tree (*Cercis siliquastrum*, see page 66), which has clusters of rose-lilac flowers around its branches.

The yellow flowers of *Laburnum* × *watereri* 'Vossii' (see page 85) appear as late spring becomes summer, the drooping racemes making an impressive show (but note that all parts of the plant are poisonous).

summer flowers

There are fewer trees that flower in summer; many are large shrubs and need specific site conditions. For impressive flowers in early to midsummer consider *Cornus kousa* (see page 69) with its numerous white flowers (strictly speaking these are bracts), which makes a stunning specimen given the right site.

Later in the summer *Eucryphia* × *nymansensis* 'Nymansay' (see page 77) is covered with beautiful single, white flowers set off by showy yellow stamens.

winter flowers

Finally, for the sheer delight of seeing flowers in the middle of winter why not consider *Prunus* × *subhirtella* (see page 107)? The white flowers are borne through the winter, and it also offers good autumn foliage.

BERRIES AND FRUITS

Fruits are often thought of as an autumn feature, although those of the cherries (*Prunus*) actually ripen in the summer. Fruits add colour and provide a natural source of food for birds but can be a nuisance when they fall on hard landscaping or paths, so consider the site carefully before you plant. *Malus* 'John Downie' (see page 91) is one of the best of the fruiting crab apples with its large yellow and red fruits. The small rowan *Sorbus vilmorinii* (see page 117) offers an attractive autumn combination of bronze-red foliage and loose clusters of berries, which change from red to pinkish-white. For colour from autumn until winter, consider *Cotoneaster* 'Hybridus Pendulus' (see page 71) with its long-lasting red berries and evergreen foliage; or *Crataegus persimilis* 'Prunifolia' (see page 75) for its combination of rich autumn colour and persistent fruit.

BARK

Tree bark becomes a feature particularly during winter when the distraction of leaves and flowers has gone. It is set off to best advantage by a solid background such as a conifer hedge, lawn or planting of evergreen perennials. Silver birch (*Betula pendula*, see page 61) is well known for its graceful habit and white stems, but for further winter colour, you can always underplant it with a carpet of evergreen perennials and early spring bulbs. Although the species itself is likely to grow too tall for a small garden, the cultivar 'Youngii' is very

suitable, and in winter the pendulous branches will be bare and expose the trunk that is screened by foliage in summer.

The paperbark maple (*Acer griseum*) will, in time, develop a peeling bark that is brown with orange beneath, and it has the bonus of good autumn colour. *A. davidii* (see page 50) has a green and white striped bark as its main feature but also offers autumn foliage and fruits. The peeling bark of *Prunus serrula* (see page 104) is a polished red-brown, a very warming sight on a cold winter day.

TRIPLE-INTEREST TREES

Amelanchier lamarckii (see page 57) has spring blossom among copper-tinted leafy shoots, black berries and then brilliant red- and orange-coloured leaves in autumn.

Arbutus unedo (see page 58) is a small evergreen tree that grows in beauty as it matures when the bark becomes an increasingly deep brown and shredded. The white flowers and strawberry-like fruits are borne at the same time in late autumn.

Below: *Acer griseum* (paperbark maple) is one of the finest multi-merit trees, with interesting winged seeds, intense autumn colour and peeling bark.

1 MAKING A CHOICE

There are so many small trees available in garden centres and through specialist suppliers that it is worth taking time to select the tree or trees that will best suit your garden. Looking for a tree that will offer year-round interest, whether in the form of structure and shape, foliage colour, interesting bark, or flowers and fruit, is only half the process. Your choice must also depend on the conditions in your garden: the soil type, the climate and aspect and, most importantly, the space you have available.

Most trees prefer deep, fairly rich, well-drained but moisture-retentive soil, and they tend to do best in neutral to slightly acid soil, although there are, of course, exceptions to this rule, which are noted in the individual descriptions in the Directory. Trees also tend to do best in good light. When they are planted in shade they do not flower or fruit as well as similar plants grown in a sunny position. Trees growing in shade all day long usually grow taller and narrower than they would do in good light.

Trees grown for their delicate foliage usually require protection from cold, drying winds, especially while they are becoming established, and those that bear flowers early in the year may also be affected by late spring frosts.

When you are selecting a tree from the ranks you see in your local nursery or from the pages of a catalogue, therefore, make sure that it is suitable for your garden. A tree planted in unfavourable conditions will never thrive and achieve its full potential and may even simply give up the unequal struggle and die.

size and shape

When choosing a tree it is essential that you select one that is appropriate for the size of your garden. Tall, fast-growing conifers, such as × *Cupressocyparis leylandii*, can quickly outgrow their allotted space and take the moisture and nutrients from the soil around them, and there are many other widely available trees that are simply not suitable for a limited area.

Consider these four factors when choosing a tree for your garden:

- size
- spread
- shape
- speed of growth

SIZE

Despite the precision with which measurements are often quoted in reference books, there is a certain amount of leeway to tree dimensions. Height and spread are often given at set periods, such as five and ten years after planting, or are expressed as ultimate heights, which can be unnecessarily off-putting, because not only are some trees slow growing and long lived but, in a garden, they may never achieve the dimensions the same tree growing in the wild would attain.

The height indicated in the Directory of Trees (pages 47–121) is the size a tree is likely to achieve in a garden setting after about 20 years. For the purposes of this book, 'small' is taken to mean a height of 10m (30ft) or less.

spread

Although its ultimate height will probably be your first concern when you are selecting a tree, you should also consider ultimate spread. A slim, upright tree, such as *Juniperus scopulorum* 'Skyrocket' (see page 83), which may eventually grow to be 6m (20ft) tall, rarely grows wider than about 60cm (2ft). A spreading tree, such as *Magnolia* × *soulangeana* (see page 86), may grow as wide as it is tall. When you are siting a tree, therefore, it is important to know how much space to leave around it.

shape

Closely connected with the spread is its ultimate shape. Many small trees can be grown as shrubs, with several stems arising from the ground. Where planting space is at a premium, however, a tree with an upright, bare trunk and a spreading canopy or crown, will allow you to grow bulbs and low-growing annuals and perennials, to bloom before the tree's leaves form dense shade.

speed of growth

Some small trees reach their full height quite quickly, whereas others, such as holly (*Ilex aquifolium*, see page 80), which may reach 25m (80ft) in the wild, grow slowly enough for their size not to be a problem for many years in a small garden.

Left: *Malus* × *purpurea* 'Lemoinei' is one of the many small flowering crab apples.

trees that remain small

These trees grow only to a fixed height as they have been grafted on to a specified rootstock. Any growth will take place in the weeping branches, but these can be easily trimmed back if need be.

Caragana arborescens 'Pendula'	**This is a shrub that has been grafted on to the top of a straight stem to form a small weeping tree.**
Cotoneaster 'Hybridus Pendulus'	**This is actually a spreading bush that has been grafted on top of a stem of an upright species, such as *C. bullatus*, to given the appearance of a small weeping tree.**
Prunus 'Kiku-shidare-zakura'	**A weeping cherry that has been grafted on to a stem of *P. avium*.**
Salix caprea 'Kilmarnock'	**This tree reaches only 2–3m (6–10ft), depending on the height of the stem on to which it was grafted.**

larger but slow-growing trees

These trees will grow to substantial heights given the right circumstances but will do so only slowly and can be pruned in the meantime.

Arbutus unedo	**This spreading tree is slow growing for about the first 15 years and takes even longer to reach its ultimate height of 4.5m (15ft).**
Malus hybrids (flowering crabs)	**The height depends on the choice of rootstock; if they are available on a dwarfing apple rootstock, such as M27, they will remain very small.**
Ilex spp. (hollies)	**Hollies are slow growing so don't be put off by ultimate height. *Ilex aquifolium* can be grown as a mophead standard. There is also the aptly named *Ilex aquifolium* 'Green Pillar', an erect form with a narrow growth habit.**

tall but narrow trees

In a small garden it is the horizontal space that is at such a premium so trees that are tall but have a narrow growth habit are particularly useful.

Juniperus scopulorum 'Skyrocket'	**The narrowest of all conifers. One tree at the Hillier Garden and Arboretum in Hampshire, UK, is 5m (16ft) high but has a diameter of only 30cm (1ft).**
Prunus 'Amanogawa'	**A small, columnar tree with erect branches.**
Ulmus minor 'Dampieri Aurea'	**An unusual elm, this tree makes a tight golden pillar that may have a spread of only 75cm (2ft) by the time it is 3m (10ft) tall.**

siting trees

As trees are a long-term feature of a garden, you want to able to reap the benefit of them as they mature rather than have to hack back or even remove them when they are in their prime simply because of a lack of foresight at the time of planting. The following headings cover the main practical points to consider. Together they sound rather off-putting, so it is worth noting that one of the best places to plant a tree in small garden is to one side of the lawn, with at least 1m (3ft) of turf removed all round for ease of maintenance. Small trees also work well in borders or near water, if the pond is netted in autumn.

- planting near boundaries
- planting near hard landscaping
- planting near buildings
- shade

PLANTING NEAR BOUNDARIES

Avoid planting trees where the branches will overhang your neighbour's garden or the highway. Plants intruding into neighbours' gardens cause many disputes, and there are rules in many countries about neighbours' rights to chop down overhanging vegetation, so such situations are best avoided. Similarly, if vegetation is blocking sightlines for pedestrians or drivers, it is dangerous and you may spoil the shape of the tree if you are forced to cut it back.

PLANTING NEAR HARD LANDSCAPING

Leaves and fallen fruits cause little problem when they drop on to a lawn or border soil as earthworms take down the leaves into the soil and fruits soon rot away. However, where the ground has hard landscaping, such as a patio or steps, fallen leaves can be a nuisance or at worst dangerous when they get wet. Avoid planting a tree near where you park your car, particularly if it has fruit, because the bird mess and staining can damage the paintwork.

Tree roots can cause damage to paths and drives. There is a risk that weedkillers used on these areas could run off down to the tree roots.

Prickly trees, such as holly (*Ilex*), can be a nuisance near a narrow but well-used path.

Right: *Juniperus communis* 'I libernica', the Irish juniper, is a good choice where you need a space-saving conifer.

PLANTING NEAR BUILDINGS

There is nothing to be gained by planting a tree near a building. Foundations can be weakened by tree roots, which can also affect drains, sewers and water supplies. Above ground, the tree will reduce the amount of light reaching the inside of the building. Routine maintenance, such as dealing with blocked gutters or painting, will all be made much harder if a tree is in the way.

Insurance companies are much more aware about the risks of trees causing subsidence in buildings these days, although most serious damage is restricted to species not covered in this book, such as weeping willows and poplars. The problem is also aggravated by soil type, with tree roots in clay soils causing the most concern.

From the tree's point of view a building is not the ideal neighbour. The soil near the foundations is likely to be poor. The tree will almost certainly develop a lop-sided shape as it will be shaded on one side, and lower branches may be physically damaged by contact with the wall.

As a rule, do not plant a tree nearer to a building than one and half times the likely height of the tree. However, if you have an established tree that is nearer than this don't worry unduly.

SHADE

Once a tree matures it may cast too much shade underneath it to support plant growth, particularly if it has a spreading habit and a dense leaf canopy. Grass in particular suffers when shaded by trees, so it is best to remove a large area and replace it with bark chips rather than persevere with the grass. Trees with small leaves or a light canopy, such as birch or *Robinia pseudoacacia* 'Frisia', cast only a light dappled shade, which offers plenty of scope for underplanting.

Right above: *Acer palmatum* var. *dissectum* is generally a bit shrubby in habit and plants tend to be mushroom-shaped when young. You can rely on a good display of autumn colour before the leaves fall.

Right: Laburnums are justifiably widely planted, and they are among the most beautiful of all trees when in full flower. The one illustrated is *L.* × *watereri*, but grow the cultivar *L.* × *w.* 'Vossii' for a really good show.

soil and site

In the wild trees are found growing in the most apparently difficult conditions, clinging to mountain sides or buffeted by strong, salt-laden winds. In a garden it is possible to provide a tree with the optimum conditions in terms of:

- soil type

- aspect

- sun and shade

SOIL TYPE

Before you buy a tree, check the pH of your soil to determine if it is acid or alkaline. Inexpensive, easy-to-use kits are widely available. Trees grown in inappropriate soil simply will not thrive: their leaves will yellow and, eventually, drop. The tree may not die, but it will never look healthy.

ASPECT

When they are first planted all trees need protection from the wind until their roots have developed sufficiently to anchor them firmly. Some trees have delicate leaves that will be torn and damaged by strong winds; grow such plants in a sheltered spot or protect with a windbreak.

SUN AND SHADE

All plants need sunlight to photosynthesize, but some trees grow well in shade or partial shade. The leaves of trees with pale green or golden-green foliage may scorch in strong sunlight, but variegated trees must be in good light if the attractive leaf variegation is to be retained.

Left: 'Thorns' of various kinds, like this *Crataegus pedicellata*, tolerate most conditions, including heavy clay soils and wet ground. Most other trees are more demanding.

plants for particular soils and sites

heavy clay soils

Abies	Magnolia
Amelanchier	Malus
Crataegus	Prunus
Ilex	Salix
Juniperus	Sorbus
Laburnum	Ulmus

Most trees take longer to establish on a heavy clay soil as it is so difficult for the roots to penetrate, so try to improve the drainage. The tree should be planted at the same level as it was in the nursery, but plant young trees on a mound of improved soil to give them a greater depth in which to root before having to cope with wet clay.

wet boggy soils

Amelanchier	Pyrus
Crataegus	Salix

Only a few trees from the Directory of Trees can cope with wet soil, the main problem being waterlogging of the roots and a lack of oxygen. In very wet, bog-like conditions only a handful of tree species will be suitable.

dry sandy soils

Betula	Juniperus
Cercis	Pyrus
Cotoneaster	Robinia
Crataegus	Sorbus
Fagus	Ulmus
Ilex aquifolium	

Trees will be slower to establish and grow in these soils, because of lack of moisture. Soluble nutrients, such as nitrogen, quickly drain away too. When planting, incorporate slow-release general fertilizers and plant the tree in a small depression so that water drains into the soil around the root zone rather than runs off.

thin chalky soils

Acer griseum	Fagus
Arbutus unedo	Juniperus
Caragana arborescens	Laburnum
	Malus
Crataegus	Prunus
	Pyrus
	Rhus

Where there is a thin layer of topsoil over chalk, many trees struggle to make decent specimens. However, a deep soil over chalk is a different matter, with most trees able to thrive. Annual additions of organic matter or ordinary topsoil to the surface can help improve a tree's chances of developing well.

cold windy sites

Betula pendula	Juniperus
	Laburnum
Crataegus	Salix
Fagus	Ulmus
Ilex aquiflorum	

Trees may need to sheltered for the first two years, either with a hedge or a temporary windbreak that filters the wind. Double-staking might be necessary (see pages 34–5). Evergreens can suffer in cold, windy sites; large-leaved specimens are also at risk of being disfigured.

coastal sites

Acer griseum	Cotoneaster
Arbutus unedo	Crataegus
	Juniperus
Ilex aquifolium	Pyrus
	Ulmus

Seaside winds carry salt spray, which can damage foliage of sensitive plants. Double-staking might be necessary (see pages 34–5).

containers

Growing trees in containers is not a new idea, but has become increasingly popular as gardens have become smaller and more use is made of patios and decked areas. Almost every tree can be grown, at least for part of its life, in a pot, and a container can stand near to a building and be used in roof gardens and courtyards, on balconies and near to doors and arches, bringing a tree much nearer to the house than would otherwise be possible. When you use containers for a tree, bear in mind:

- type of tree
- grouping containers
- size of container

TYPES OF TREE

Growing a tree in a container restricts its root run, and the overall height and spread of the tree will, eventually, be reduced. In general, slow-growing trees and those that have a reasonable degree of drought-tolerance will fare best.

Trees that do not look too lanky and bare at the base are best, although you may be able to overcome this by planting bulbs or even a groundcover plant in the container to hide the base of the trunk. Remember, too, that it is important to choose a tree that will be in proportion with the size and shape of its container.

Left above: Many Japanese maples make ideal container trees, although they can be expensive and need careful looking after, especially when young. The one illustrated is *Acer palmatum* var. *dissectum*.

Left: The various forms of *Acer palmatum* make excellent container trees, but young specimens should be given a sheltered position as young growth can be damaged by late frosts and cold spring winds.

grouping and arranging pots

When grouping plants together in pots, the effect is more successful if you grow each one as a single subject in its own pot and then group the pots together, rather than trying to grow a mixture of plants in one large container. However, if you have only limited planting space, a large tub with a tree underplanted with bulbs and ivy can work well.

When it comes to arranging container plants the same principles apply as for border plantings. Choose a permanent 'backbone' of woody subjects, including both deciduous and evergreens type, then look for contrasts of form and foliage to provide the impact rather than rely on flowering or autumn fruit alone. Use smaller pots full of bedding or bulbs to add seasonal highlights and remove them from the scene once they are past their best.

A pair of containers standing either side of an entrance or at the top of steps works well with formal shapes like upright conifers or clipped evergreens such as holly.

CONTAINER SIZE

It is important that the roots are restricted but not pot-bound, so in the early years you should gradually move trees on from the pots they were purchased in into containers up to 45cm (18in) in diameter.

The final container should be at least 60cm (2ft) in diameter and depth. Wooden half-barrels are often used successfully, and there is a growing range of attractive plastic pots. Terracotta is very expensive in these larger sizes and there is always the risk it will not be frost-resistant despite claims to the contrary. Any container used will need drainage holes to prevent waterlogging of the compost, and it's worth raising the pot off the ground slightly.

Below. Most kinds of birch (*Betula*) are likely to grow too large for a small garden, but a very large container will restrict their growth. Choose one trained into a multi-stemmed tree for most impact.

trees for containers

Amelanchier lamarckii

Caragana arborescens 'Pendula'

Cotoneaster 'Hybridus Pendulus'

Crataegus laevigata 'Paul's Scarlet'

Ilex aquifolium

Juniperus scopulorum 'Skyrocket'

Laburnum × *watereri* 'Vossii'
(for a limited time)

*Malus floribunda**

M. 'John Downie'*

*M. tschonoskii**

Robinia pseudoacacia 'Frisia'
(for a limited time)

Prunus 'Amanogawa'

P. 'Kiku-shidare-zakura'

P. × *subhirtella*

Pyrus salicifolia 'Pendula'

Salix caprea 'Kilmarnock'

Sorbus vilmorinii

* Grow only *Malus* that have been grafted on to a very dwarfing rootstock in container.

Trees are grown and offered for sale in two main forms: as bare-rooted plants or as container-grown plants in pots. **Bare-rooted trees** are grown by a nursery in open ground, then lifted during the dormant season. The soil falls away from the roots, leaving them exposed; there is some damage to the roots during lifting and handling. However, if the plant has a decent amount of root, this is protected from drying out with damp newspaper or similar material; the plant is handled with care and despatched promptly to the customer. Such plants establish well and are much cheaper than container-grown plants. Being lighter, it is more feasible to buy these from specialist growers who will post them to you.

Larger trees, especially conifers or evergreens over 1.5m (5ft) can be offered as 'rootballed' trees. These are grown in a similar way to bare-rooted trees but dug up with soil round the roots, which are wrapped in hessian or plastic.

Most trees on sale in garden centres will be ready-trained and container-grown. If you buy by post the trees are much more likely to be younger and bare-rooted. (For more details see pages 26–9.)

where to buy trees

Trees can be obtained from several different sources and in a number of different ways, each of which has its advantages and disadvantages:

- general garden outlet
- specialist tree nursery
- mail-order and internet

Below: It is a good sign if the trees are clearly displayed, well labelled and securely supported. But don't forget that most garden centres are happy to order a particular tree if it is not on display.

GENERAL GARDEN OUTLETS

A typical garden centre will carry a fairly modest selection of tree species, although most of these will be suitable for a small or medium-sized garden. The trees will already have been trained and pruned, either to a full standard size, with a clear stem of 1.8–2.1m (6–7ft), or half-standard size, with a clear stem of 1.2–1.5m (4–5ft). You may find that there is a wider range of conifers, with a choice of young plants or more mature specimens.

Container-grown trees will be on sale all year round, but the widest choice and freshest plants will usually be available in spring. In general, avoid buying trees in the height of summer because the roots can become very stressed in the compost at this time.

Most garden centres buy in their trees from wholesale growers, so it is important to choose an outlet that has a rapid turnover of stock. Avoid plants with faded labels, split pots, weedy compost and poor, misshapen foliage, which may indicate that the trees that have been sitting in their pots for more than two growing seasons. When plants are standing out on display for more than a growing season, they run out of the nutrients and moisture in the small volume of compost, which will lead to wilting, premature flowering and discoloured foliage.

SPECIALIST NURSERY

A nursery that specializes in trees will offer a greater range of species and sizes than a garden centre. Such nurseries vary from keen amateurs, with a small nursery in their garden, to large wholesalers, which supply garden centres. Look for advertisements in gardening journals and magazines or visit garden shows, where you may be able to see examples of the trees you are considering for your own garden. You could also check with friends, who may be able to recommend a good nursery or tell you which ones to avoid.

Nurseries that specialize in growing only trees should be able to offer the widest choice of species at various stages of growth. Some supply young, bare-rooted plants by mail order, but they may offer only a limited range of species, including native trees. Plants are likely to be available only during the dormant season (autumn and winter), so you must be prepared to plant your tree as soon as you get it, which may not always be convenient.

Some suppliers offer mature specimens. Their main customers are landscape and garden designers, who want large, one-off specimens for specific purposes, but many will also supply to the public. Typically, the containers will be around 45cm (18in) across and will support a tree 2.1m (7ft) or more tall. Such trees may be around ten years old. As the stock is all grown in containers the outlets are open all year round and are not dependent on the weather. Most suppliers will produce catalogues, but it is preferable wherever possible to visit the outlet to check the tree yourself before purchase.

Although it may be tempting to buy the largest possible tree you can afford, remember that large trees are difficult to transport and plant and they are slow to establish. A smaller, young tree will not only be less expensive but will also soon catch up with a mature specimen as its root system establishes more quickly.

MAIL ORDER AND INTERNET

Using a catalogue or the internet to order a tree that is delivered to your door can be an easy and convenient option if you follow a few basic guidelines.

Most orders are processed and delivered during the dormant season, but it is usually best to order well in advance, as soon as the catalogue is available, because orders are processed in rotation and delay may mean that your order cannot be met because stocks have run out. It is sometimes possible to specify delivery time on the order form, and some suppliers will supply substitutes if wished. You should also let the supplier know if you will not be available to accept an order at a particular time and where the delivery can be left if you are not at home to receive it.

Unpack the tree as soon as it is delivered. If you cannot plant it immediately, a bare-rooted tree should be potted up into a large container or heeled in at the back of a border to protect the roots.

If the tree is left unopened in warm, wet conditions it might start into growth but will be drawn and leggy through lack of light.

Above: Always unpack mail order plants on arrival. If you can't plant them where you want them straight away, plant them temporarily in a spare piece of ground, or pot up small specimens.

choosing a good specimen

It pays to take extra care choosing a good-quality tree. The main types are:

- container-grown
- bare-rooted
- conifers
- grafted trees

CONTAINER-GROWN

Look for a tree with a straight, even stem or trunk. The top growth should be balanced and well-shaped. Where trees are displayed close together, pull out several to judge the shape. Foliage should look healthy and vigorous, with no widespread unnatural yellow or red tinges. Inspect the young foliage for pests and diseases.

It is important that the tree has established roots in the pot, which usually takes about 12 weeks during the growing season. Check by lifting the tree up by the trunk – a reasonable rootball should hold the tree in its pot.

At the other end of the spectrum, avoid a tree that has been in the same pot for several seasons and has become pot-bound. Weedy or split pots, faded labels and roots growing out of the drainage holes into the gravel beds are all warning signs. A pot-bound plant will have a very tangled root system with the main roots encircling the pot. When the tree is planted out into open ground, the roots will not spread out to anchor the plant through a well-developed root system. Also, the roots can become so entangled with each other they can't take up water and nutrients efficiently, leading to loss of vigour of the whole plant. Ideally, do not buy a pot-bound tree, but if you do, cut out the spiralling roots so that new ones will grow outwards.

BARE-ROOTED

There is not the same opportunity to inspect bare-rooted specimens as these are usually despatched by mail order. The interval between

Above: If growing apples in pots, be sure to buy one grown on a very dwarfing rootstock. Let your supplier know that you want to grow it in a container and ask for a dwarfing rootstock.

lifting from the ground and replanting should be as short as possible, during which time the roots should be protected with damp newspaper or straw or in a polythene bag, and the tree kept cool but frost-free.

CONIFERS

Look for a symmetrical shape that is well-clothed with healthy foliage. Avoid trees with bare patches or browning of the foliage.

Phytophthora is a serious, often fatal, fungal disease that attacks conifers, so avoid infected trees. It is noticeable as a general browning of the foliage, extending from the base upwards. As it is spread by contaminated water, do not buy conifers that are left to sit in water or that have a thick layer of liverwort on the compost surface.

When choosing between rootballed conifers, opt for the one with the largest rootball and where the covering is secure and intact.

GRAFTED TREES

If a tree has been grafted on to a different rootstock, the union should have healed well with no more than a slight bend in it. Ornamental trees are usually grafted near the ground but pendulous trees are grafted higher up the stem. Look out for and remove suckers growing from the rootstock.

planting container-grown trees

The traditional wisdom has been to mix in plenty of organic soil improver with the soil when planting a tree, and slow-release fertilizers such as bonemeal were often suggested as well. Many gardeners feel comfortable with this advice, given the price of trees and that this is the only opportunity thereafter to improve the soil without damaging the tree roots. However, in recent years a number of studies on tree and shrub planting have shown that mulching and reducing competition from nearby vegetation, such as grass and weeds, contributes more to successful tree establishment than soil improvement does.

Above: A tree planted in an exposed site should be staked for a year or two until its roots have had a chance to establish themselves firmly.

PEAT SUBSTITUTES

Many gardeners now wish to reduce their use of peat as a planting medium. Peat-free substitutes are increasingly available, although they are usually more expensive than peat-based equivalents. There have also been, albeit unofficial, safety concerns over the use of bonemeal. So the soil improvement and fertilizer additions are really a matter of personal conviction. The key point is to give the tree a chance to establish without competition for the first two years and to use mulches that will suppress weeds and help to retain moisture.

ENSURING PLANTING SUCCESS

Container-grown plants make life easier as the planting season is much more flexible. They have their own root system encased in compost, so they can be planted at any time when the soil is workable. Provided the tree was not pot-bound, it should be more successful at establishing itself than an equivalent bare-rooted tree.

The key point is to water plants thoroughly before planting so the compost is fully wetted, and to dig a large planting hole to take the rootball comfortably.

Planting a container-grown tree

1 Water the plant thoroughly and allow to drain while you are preparing the hole. Remove any turf or weeds, to create a clear area 1m (3ft) in diameter.

2 Dig out a large hole, twice the size of the tree's rootball. Put the topsoil to one side. If you are using soil improvers and fertilizers mix them in with the topsoil.

3 Trees over 1.2m (4ft) can benefit from staking. It can be done at this stage to avoid root damage by inserting a stake just off-centre on the side that gets the wind (see pages 34–5).

Remove the tree from its container and gently tease out any roots growing around in a circle with a handfork. If they have become too woody to do this, cut them off with secateurs.

4 Add some of the topsoil to the bottom of the hole. Position the tree in the hole and use a bamboo cane or piece of wood to check the planting depth – the tree needs to be planted at the depth it was growing in the pot. Adjust the depth by adding or removing topsoil from under the rootball. This is fiddly but worthwhile, so spend time getting it right, but don't let the rootball dry out in the meantime.

Once the tree is at the correct level, backfill with topsoil, firming it down gently with your foot as you go along. The aim is to remove any large air pockets and ensure the roots make contact with soil, but not to compress the soil too hard.

6 Water the tree in well. Lay down a circle of sheet mulch and disguise with a thin layer of chipped bark. In areas prone to dry spells a length of pipe can be laid around the rootball with one end open at the soil surface. During dry spells, water can be poured down the open end direct to the rootball.

5 Trees that are to be staked need a tree tie to secure the tree to the stake. If necessary, protect the young bark from rabbits or other damage with a tree guard.

planting bare-rooted trees

Bare-rooted trees should be planted only during the dormant season and this should be completed as soon as possible after lifting to prevent drying and damage to the roots.

- when to plant
- ensuring planting success
- compost for trees in containers

WHEN TO PLANT

Deciduous trees are best lifted and planted after they have shed their leaves. Evergreens are better planted either earlier in the autumn or in mid-spring when their roots are active so can replace the moisture lost by the foliage. Deciduous trees, such as magnolias, with thick fleshy roots that are prone to rotting in cold, wet soils, are often better when planted at evergreen planting time.

ENSURING PLANTING SUCCESS

Between lifting and planting, protect the tree from cold winds or strong sunshine. Keep it in a cool but frost-free place, such as a porch, greenhouse, garage or shed. Keep the roots slightly moist – use damp straw or a plastic bag. If the tree cannot be planted for more than a few days, place the roots in a bucket of moist peat or compost.

   If you have a lot of bare-rooted plants and no time to plant them out, then 'heel' them in. This means digging a trench in a sheltered place with well-drained soil drained. Set the plants at an angle and cover the roots with moist soil.

COMPOST FOR TREES IN CONTAINERS

A soil-based compost, such as a John Innes type, will add weight to the container, useful with a top-heavy tree. It also maintains its physical structure better outside year after year, unlike peat-based composts which can lose their structure in winter rains unless mulched or protected. Use peat-based multi-purpose compost for easy-to-manoeuvre pots or if you are prepared to repot regularly.

1 New plastic or wood containers may need drainage holes drilled in them. Old containers will need scrubbing out with hot soapy water to prevent carry-over of pests and diseases.

2 Cover the drainage holes with old crocks to prevent the compost washing through or add a 2.5cm (1in) or more layer of gravel. Stand the container on bricks or special 'feet' to aid drainage and prevent staining of the patio. Position the container in its final site before planting. Fill the pot with compost.

3 Small standard trees may need a stake, which can be inserted before planting. Take the tree out of its pot and plant so that the soil mark on the stem is about 5cm (2in) below the container rim.

4 Firm the compost down gently as you go along using your hands. Mulch to reduce the need to water: chipped bark, gravel, slate or even pebbles all work well.

planting rootballed trees

Keep the plant wrapped up until the last possible moment to protect the roots. Dig a planting hole about twice the size of the rootball. Set the topsoil to one side; if you are using soil improvers they can be mixed in. Place the tree in the hole, remove wrapping, allowing the soil to fall away into the hole. Pull the wrapping out from under the tree and dispose of it. Backfill the hole with compost, firm gently and water well.

Above: It is worth investing in an attractive container so that your potted tree makes a pleasing feature from the moment it is planted.

stakes and supports

There are a lot of misconceptions about staking trees, perhaps because of the examples seen in parks and other amenity areas. There are several approaches to staking which vary depending on the type of tree.

- purpose of staking a tree
- staking methods
- disadvantages

the purpose of staking a tree

A stake holds the roots firm in the soil until new ones can grow and anchor themselves – it is not about holding the stem rigidly in place. Staking is essentially a short-term helping hand for two or three growing seasons, not a permanent fixture. There is no need to treat the stake with preservative; in fact, it will be easier to remove if it has started to rot at the base.

staking methods

Tall stakes are often used, but research has shown that short stakes, with no more than 30–45cm (1–1½ft) above ground, are better for the development of the tree stem in the long term. A tree stem needs to be moved gently backwards and forwards by the wind to strengthen it. When the stem is held firmly in place by a tall stake it doesn't get the chance to thicken and develop, and so is more likely to snap or fall over in a strong wind than an unstaked tree that is used to bending. Staking should only be used where necessary – with trees over 1.2m (4ft) when planted or on exposed sites, and then only as a short-term measure.

To minimize root damage, particularly for container-grown trees, it is best to insert the stake before planting. A stake 1m (3ft) long can be used with 60cm (2ft) driven into the ground and the rest above. If a young tree was not staked when planted but needs one, drive it in to the ground at a 45 degree angle, so it leans into the wind.

The tree should be attached to the stake using a proprietary tree tie (sometimes called buckler and spacer ties) as they are designed to stop the tree rubbing against the stake and can be adjusted easily. The tie will need to be loosened as the girth of the tree increases, so remember to check it at the end of the growing season.

Large trees can be staked with two or three stakes, either opposite each other or spread around the trunk. Given that the rootball will be bigger, the stakes will be further from the stem, so use heavy-duty ties and nail them to the stake.

When trees have been raised with unusually thin stems, as may be the case with some types of *Malus*, the stems *do* need some support in the early years. Either support them with a bamboo cane so the stem can move in the wind and thicken up, or use a tall stake for a single growing season, then cut this down and use it as a short stake for the second season. Finally, remove it for the third growing season.

DISADVANTAGES

One argument for not staking a tree at all is that it is unnecessary; after all, nature grows trees successfully without providing stakes. Young trees, such as those you might buy from a specialist nursery, and those under about 1.2m (4ft) tall, should not need staking at all. A stake can damage the tree by rubbing against it or the tie can strangle a tree if it is not regularly loosened, so once staked, more checking is needed. Incorrect staking can make a tree more, not less, vulnerable to wind rock. Therefore, use staking only for trees that are taller than about 1.2m (4ft) when first planted or those that are in especially exposed sites, and even then regard it only as a short-term measure.

Right: If planting a fairly large tree, it may be advisable to use this kind of staking to hold the tree secure until it has rooted well into the surrounding soil. The stakes can then be removed.

3 TREE CARE

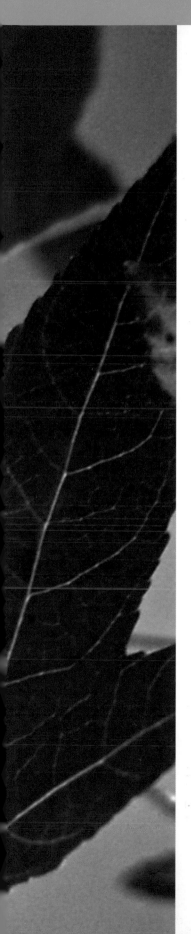

Despite the impact trees have on the garden, most require **minimal care** compared with cultivating smaller plants such as bedding or perennials. You are spared the annual ritual of preparing seedbeds, waiting for the last spring frosts and nurturing small plants against relentless slug attack. For the most part, tree care operates to a more relaxed timetable, and checks are made either in the spring or during the dormant season.

The **essentials** you need to know to get your tree off to a **successful start** are covered in the following section of the book. Many of the techniques, such as formative pruning, may be unfamiliar to you, but they are straightforward if you understand why they are done. An interesting aspect of tree care is that new ways of doing things are constantly coming to light as research into forestry and commercial tree planting finds its application in the garden.

To care for your tree and protect it from unexpected events it is worth looking at it regularly. For example, newly planted trees often get lifted out of the ground after a spell of hard frost, and it is important to firm them gently back in position with your feet before the roots dry out. Evergreens or deciduous trees with young spring growth in exposed positions are best protected with a windbreak webbing screen against cold winds, and you need to keep an eye on this to make sure it is still secure.

the early years

Once a tree has been planted the key tasks in the early years are watering, feeding and weed control. Many of these tasks can be combined by appropriate mulching techniques.

- watering
- feeding
- mulching

WATERING

Where the soil remains moist you may not need to water, particularly if the tree has a good root system and was planted and mulched correctly. But check regularly for the first couple of years.

During dry spells, or where the ground is very free-draining, such as a sandy or chalky soil, some extra watering will be needed. The most efficient way to water is to apply a reasonable amount – 14–40 litres to 1 sq m (3–8 gallons to 1 sq yd) of ground surrounding the tree – once a week rather than a light sprinkle every day. Water should be applied steadily, allowing time for it to soak into the ground before more is added. If you use a hose, be careful that the force of the stream does not wash away the soil.

To target water directly to the tree roots, insert a pipe nearby at the time of planting. Water can then be poured down this pipe using a funnel, exactly to where it is needed. This method is good for expensive trees or those inaccessible to a hose. A number of different pipes have been tried, from so called leaky hoses to tubes used for washing machines. Remember to cover the open end when not in use to prevent it gathering debris. Automatic irrigation systems are a possibility too, but as a long-term measure they are more appropriate to trees in containers.

FEEDING

A tree growing in a reasonable garden soil (such as one that was previously cultivated with plenty of organic matter) does not need any additional fertilizer. Extra fertilizer could be beneficial on very free-draining ground such as dry, sandy soils or unimproved chalky soils, as water passes through quickly, taking soluble nutrients such as nitrogen with it. In such instances apply a general fertilizer with roughly equal amounts of nitrogen, phosphorus and potassium, ideally one that releases the nitrogen slowly.

Fertilizer is usually applied as a powder or granules around the tree base in spring before mulching. Apply when the soil is moist or water well afterwards as dry fertilizer can scorch roots.

Mulching with well-rotted organic matter, such as cocoa shells, rotted farmyard manure or garden compost, will supply some nutrients.

MULCHING

A mulch suppresses weeds and helps keep the ground moist by reducing the evaporation from the soil surface. Mulch is best applied in early or mid-spring (make sure the area is weed-free first).

Choose a material to fit the setting, from gravel, chipped bark, cocoa shells, manure or leafmould, laid at least 5cm (2in) thick, or use black polythene, woven polypropylene or even newspaper.

Left: Vulnerable plants may benefit from wind protection such as hessian or horticultural fleece while young, but where animals such as deer or rabbits are likely to be the problem wire-netting may be more appropriate.

pruning and training

There are a number of different reasons for pruning trees, and many trees will need different types of pruning at different ages.

- routine pruning for shape or size
- formative pruning
- pruning out diseased or dead branches
- removing suckers

ROUTINE PRUNING

Unlike most flowering trees and shrubs, established trees need little or no routine pruning except where there are dead, damaged or diseased branches to tackle. However, particularly in a small garden, you might want a tree that has been shaped in its early years – this is known as formative pruning. For example, if it is left to its own devices, *Amelanchier lamarckii* forms a multi-stemmed, large shrub, but formative pruning to encourage a single stem can produce a small tree with a rounded crown.

FORMATIVE PRUNING

How much formative pruning you need to do depends on the age of tree, how much was already done before you bought it, and what shape of tree you want. For container-grown trees around 1.8m (6ft) high, as you might find in a garden centre, some training will have already been done to form the stem and head. It is then a matter of choosing what shape is appropriate for the species (see the individual entries in the Directory of Trees for more details) and following the instructions shown on page 40.

pruning young trees

When you buy young trees (often called whips or maidens) from a hedging supplier or tree specialist you might have to do more of the formative pruning yourself. Start at ground level and remove two-thirds of the sideshoots but leave any leaf rosettes near the stem. In the second year repeat this process. From then on prune for shape (see above).

pruning established trees

Little routine pruning is needed once a framework has been formed, but it is worth pruning out any dead, damaged or diseased branches as they can spread problems to the rest of the tree as well as spoil the appearance.

Below: Most trees require very little pruning, and the shape of conifers, in particular, can be spoilt by hard pruning. For that reason it's important to choose suitable varieties in the first place, bearing in mind their likely eventual size

feathered trees

These have a leading shoot clothed with sideshoots. During the dormant season cut back the sideshoots to within 5–10cm (2–4in) of the main stem. If the side branches are overcrowded, remove the weakest ones.

standard trees

Remove the sideshoots so there is a clear stem up to the head of the tree. Any leaf clusters that grow from the stem without forming a shoot should be left. Remove any other dominant shoot that threatens to compete with the leader. Small branches can simply be sawn through, but larger ones should be removed in stages.

multi-stemmed trees

Trees with attractive bark are often grown this way. Specimens may be available already trained, or you can prune back hard a very young (maiden) tree to encourage two or three shoots to grow out from the base.

weeping trees

Formative pruning has to create a clear stem tall enough to allow the branches to hang attractively, but as this is part of the selling feature most trees will be purchased with this pruning already done. If the weeping branches will benefit from trimming to improve the symmetry, cut out any inward-facing or upward-facing ones to create the best shape. To control the height, cut out the central leader above a branch and prune out any leader that forms afterwards.

removing a branch

To help form a longer clear stem on a young tree, cut some of the lower shoots back to the main stem.

Small branches can simply be sawn through, but larger ones should be removed in stages.

REMOVING SUCKERS

Where a tree has been grafted on to a different rootstock there is always the risk that the rootstock will produce its own shoots. These suckers should be removed promptly as they will sap the strength from the main tree and could even outgrow it. Shoots may appear just beneath the graft union or they may come up from the roots some distance from the tree. Cut or pull the suckers off as close to their origin as possible and rub out any regrowth as soon as it appears.

WHEN TO PRUNE

Prune in late autumn to winter. Some trees like *Acer*, *Betula* and *Prunus* release a lot of sap when cut, so for these the best time is mid-summer. Evergreens are best pruned in late summer.

pests and diseases

Most gardeners will be unfortunate if they have to cope with anything worse than slugs eating tender, young shoots or colonies of aphids in spring, and trees are, in general, better able to overcome and resist pests and diseases than other plants, partly because of their size and longevity and partly because of the protective barrier formed by the bark. A garden containing a wide range of different plant types will quickly establish a balance, in which pests and diseases find it difficult to take hold.

REMEDIAL ACTION

It is far better to prevent an outbreak of disease or pest infestation than to have to get rid of it. Make it difficult for a tree to succumb to problems by giving it the best possible growing conditions. Ensure it receives sufficient water and nutrients for it to grow sturdily and strongly. Trees are most at risk if the bark is damaged, which may create an entry point for pests or diseases. Use shears rather than a strimmer to cut grass around the trunk – it may take longer, but you are far less likely to damage the bark.

Some of the most common pests and diseases are described on pages 42–3. If you prefer not to use chemicals in your garden, attracting birds, to eat insect pests, and using sticky bands around the trunk of a tree may be sufficient protection.

Below: By the time the fruiting bodies of honey fungus (*Armillaria mellea*) can be seen the disease is already well established. To confirm diagnosis make the checks suggested on page 43.

pests

Symptom Colonies of greenfly, blackfly or even pinkish bugs around leaves and young shoots

Probable cause Aphids

Action Pinch out affected leaves if they can be reached safely; small trees could be sprayed with a suitable aphid killer

Symptom Ragged holes in young leaves

Probable cause Caterpillars

Action Pick off any you can reach – spraying in spring often works well as their soft bodies are vulnerable to chemicals. To avoid problems, grease bands can be placed around the trunk in mid-autumn to prevent female moths climbing up

Symptom Small reddish growths on the leaves. Look alarming but are usually harmless

Probable cause Gall mites

Action Pick off affected leaves or wait until the leaves fall and then burn them

Symptom Speckling or bronzing of young leaves from spring onwards

Probable cause Red spider mites

Action Spray young trees after flowering with a suitable insecticide

Symptom Colonies of brown, yellow or white scales on older wood

Probable cause Scale insects

Action Brush them off with warm, soapy water. Use a suitable insecticide in spring

diseases

Symptom Shallow patches on the bark of *Prunus* species in autumn/winter. By the spring there might be a brown gum oozing out

Probable cause Bacterial canker

Action Prune out affected branches and spray with a copper-based fungicide

Symptom Toadstools that look like small shelves grow from the trunk or branches

Probable cause Bracket fungi

Action Cut off affected branches. Where the fungus affects the trunk try to cut the fungus out, removing any rotting wood if practicable

Symptom Branches dying back and red pustules seen

Probable cause Coral spot

Action Cut out dead wood, and as the fungus can spread to live wood too cut back to about 15cm (6in) below the disease. Burn the prunings

Symptom Branches dying back, leaves turning brown and withering. Cankers may also be present

Probable cause Fireblight

Action Prune out diseased wood 60cm (2ft) back into healthy tissue. Burn the prunings

Symptom Oval cankers on the trunk and branches, often shrunken with the bark drying in rings

Probable cause Fungal canker

Action Cut out and burn affected material. Spray with copper-based fungicide in late summer

Symptom Leaves turning yellow and dying off prematurely. Sometimes, honey-coloured toadstools at the base of the trunk. White, fluffy growth beneath the bark at the base of the tree and perhaps black 'bootlaces' by which the fungus spreads, in the soil or under the bark

Probable cause Honey fungus

Action This is a serious disease for which there is no cure so the tree and its roots will have to be removed and burned. Do not replant trees or shrubs on the site for at least a year, and thereafter replant with those that are not susceptible

Symptom Stunted with yellow foliage and dieback. It is most likely on very wet soils

Probable cause Phytophthora

Action Remove and burn the tree and its roots

Symptom White powdery coating on leaves and stems

Probable cause Powdery mildew

Action Remove badly infected shoots and spray with a suitable fungicide, repeating if necessary

Symptom Brown, orange or yellow spots on leaves in summer.

Probable cause Rust

Action Pick off and burn affected leaves. The tree can be sprayed with a suitable fungicide.

Symptom Green blotches on the leaves, which fall early. Blister-like pimples on young shoots, cracks and scabs on the bark.

Probable cause Scab

Action Cut out affected growth and burn. Spraying at bud stage is worthwhile if you do it regularly. To prevent problems clear up fallen leaves in winter.

Symptom The leaves have a silvery appearance, and a purple fungus may grow on dead wood. Wood may show brown or purple staining when moistened. This particularly affects Prunus species.

Probable cause Silver leaf

Action Cut out the branches to 60cm (2ft) below the stain, then use a wound sealant.

caring for trees in containers

While any tree you grow in a container will need more attention than the same species grown in the open ground to keep it in tip-top condition, most of the basic care, such as pruning and spraying, is often more manageable.

- watering and feeding
- winter care
- repotting

WATERING AND FEEDING

Growing a tree permanently in a container will restrict the spread of its roots so you will need to water and feed during the growing season throughout its life, not just in the early years.

A tree on a hot sunny patio may need watering twice a day in summer, so it is worth looking at ways to make this easier. Mulching each spring is particularly worthwhile, and using material such as gravel will also help to keep the rootball cool. Where there are numerous pots to water, or if you are often away, a simple automatic watering system or capillary matting could be the answer.

The compost will supply enough nutrients for only four to six weeks after planting, so after that you will need to add extra fertilizer.

As a matter of routine, each spring remove any old mulch and the top 5cm (2in) layer of compost with a handfork or trowel. Replace with fresh multi-purpose or potting compost mixed with a general balanced fertilizer, or better still a modern slow-release fertilizer. Water in well and add the annual mulch.

Liquid feeds can be used instead of top-dressing or as a supplement to it later in the season. There are various formulations – to encourage flowers and fruits a tomato feed can be used. Follow the instructions for the correct dose: if the concentration is too strong the roots could be scorched. It is better to apply a dilute

Above: A wide range of trees can be grown in pots provided the container is large. Even Japanese cherries, like this shapely tree, can be used. The root restriction will help to keep the plant small.

liquid feed little and often rather than large doses infrequently.

WINTER CARE

Plants in containers are more susceptible to frost damage to the roots than plants in the ground. The larger the container the less susceptible it is to temperature changes, and some materials, such as wooden barrels, offer more protection than, say, plastic or terracotta, but if there is any danger it is best to protect the plant. You may be able to move the pot to somewhere more sheltered for the winter, but an alternative is to wrap the outside of the pot in several layers of bubble wrap or straw matting. Grouping several containers together will also afford some protection in cold weather.

Heavy winter rains can cause the compost to become waterlogged, so try to provide protection as it is the effect of frozen waterlogged compost that can be fatal to the roots.

REPOTTING

After about four or five years you might notice a decline in health and vigour of the tree. This is a sign that it needs repotting into a larger container. A good time of year to do this is early to mid-spring, so that the tree is ready for the new growing season. With larger specimens or heavy containers it's worth getting help. Lay the container on its side: while one person holds it steady, the other can ease the tree out.

Use a handfork to tease out the roots so they are not so congested, and dislodge some of the old compost. Cut off any over-long or spiralling roots with secateurs. If it's not possible to pot the tree into a large container, then trim the whole rootball to reduce its size slightly and dislodge as much of the old compost as possible – the tree can then go back into its original container. Replant, putting in crocks or gravel as before and using fresh compost.

Below: Even quite tall specimens can be grown in very large containers, and the effect can be dramatic.

The ornamental trees described in this directory are all suitable for small gardens. Most will not grow taller than about 10m (30ft), but even those that, in the wild, would grow comparatively large, can be kept to manageable proportions in a garden by regular pruning.

These trees, recommended for their form, attractive foliage or for their fruit or flowers, are largely trouble free and, if advice about soil type and aspect is followed, can be planted with confidence. Many should be available in most good garden centres, although for some less well-known cultivars, it may be necessary to go to a specialist outlet. Because trees are permanent additions to your garden, it is worth taking time and trouble to find the plant you want and one that will suit your garden's conditions.

hardiness zones

Most of the trees mentioned in this book are tough and able to withstand low temperatures, but if you live in a cold part of the world it's best to make sure the trees you choose are likely to survive. Each tree entry has been given a hardiness zone, so if in doubt check with the table below. These are the average annual minimum temperatures.

1 **Below -45.6ºC**
(-50ºF)

2a **-45.85 to -42.8ºC**
(-50 to -45ºF)

2b **-42.7 to -40ºC**
(-45 to -40ºF)

3a **-39.9 to -37.3ºC**
(-40 to -35ºF)

3b **-37.2 to -34.5ºC**
(-35 to -30ºF)

4a **-34.4 to -31.7ºC**
(-30 to -25ºF)

4b **-31.6 to -28.9ºC**
(-25 to -20ºF)

5a **-28.8 to -26.2ºC**
(-20 to -15ºF)

5b **-26.1 to -23.4ºC**
(-15 to -10ºF)

6a **-23.3 to -20.6ºC**
(-10 to -5ºF)

6b **-20.5 to -17.8ºC**
(-5 to 0ºF)

7a **-17.7 to -15ºC**
(0 to +5ºF)

7b **-14.9 to -12.3ºC**
(5 to 10ºF)

Abies koreana

If you have doubts about the value of conifers, grow this one. Although quite large ultimately, it is slow growing and bears its large, wonderfully striking cones while still a very small tree. This evergreen is full of elegance, with that hint of grandeur that many other small trees lack.

SLOW GROWTH

Where conditions suit this impressive conifer from the Korean peninsula, it may ultimately exceed the height of most of the other trees in this book, but it is slow growing and in most gardens is unlikely to grow taller than about 10m (30ft), even after many years. After ten years it may have attained only 1.8m (6ft).

This conifer almost always attracts favourable comment because of its shape and stature, even when young, but especially so when the cylindrical cones appear.

ATTRACTIVE COLOUR

Close examination of the leaves (needles) will show that they are a dark, glossy green above but gleaming silvery-white below. It's a combination that's difficult to describe, but the two-tone effect is very striking, and coupled with the tree's neat habit it creates a very pleasing overall appearance. It's attractive all year round, but likely to be valued especially in winter when the majority of trees are denuded and stark.

PLEASING SHAPE

Young trees soon begin to take on a conical shape, and by the time they are perhaps ten years old the cone-shaped profile is especially pleasing, with the trunk clothed almost to ground level.

INTERESTING CONES

It's undoubtedly the cones that make this one of the most desirable of the medium-sized conifers. They're large and conspicuous and appear on young trees – much sooner than on most conifers. This also means they're more likely to be at eye level rather than above head height.

The cylindrical cones, about 10cm (4in) long and 2.5cm (1in) across, are green to violet-purple at first, turning brown later.

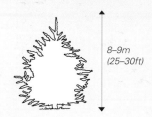

8–9m
(25–30ft)

KEY FACTS

SOIL
Ideally deep and moisture-retentive. Unlikely to do well on dry, shallow soils.

SITE
Best in a sunny, open position.

HARDINESS
Zone 5a

MAINTENANCE
Little needed, although it may develop a poor shape if cramped by neighbouring trees or shrubs.

BUYING TIP
You should be able to buy this as a container-grown plant in most good garden centres. Choose one that has a pleasing symmetrical shape with branches evenly distributed.

Left: *Abies koreana* is grown mainly for its attractive cones. These are produced even while the tree is young, sometimes on specimens less than 1m (3ft) tall.

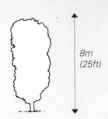

8m
(25ft)

KEY FACTS

SOIL
Best on moist but well-drained ground.

SITE
Best in full sun, but will grow well in light shade.

HARDINESS
Zone 6a

MAINTENANCE
Little required.

BUYING TIP
Although this is not a rare tree, you may have to go to a specialist grower to buy one. If you want to appreciate the beautiful bark sooner rather than later, consider buying a fairly large specimen.

Acer davidii

Snakebark maples are fascinating trees with interesting bark that often becomes a talking-point. They are grown primarily for the year-round interest provided by their bark and for autumn foliage colour. Several other acers in addition to *A. davidii* have similar interesting bark.

SLOW GROWTH

Acer davidii, one of the best snakebark maples, is native to central China and was named after the French missionary, Abbé David, who found it. In ideal conditions, and given sufficient time, it can become a medium-sized tree, but in most gardens it will remain small enough to qualify for inclusion here.

The greenish bark has fascinating vertical striations, which with a little imagination can be likened to a snake's skin. The green leaves are unlobed, unlike those of most acers, and are borne on reddish stalks; in autumn the foliage usually turns yellow before falling.

BEAUTIFUL BARK

A. davidii is grown primarily for its attractive bark, so place it where this feature can be appreciated in winter. The striations usually begin to appear on wood that's at least two years old and look best once the tree has a trunk with a reasonable girth.

FLOWERS AND FRUIT

The yellowish mid-spring flowers are inconspicuous, but the green-winged seeds ('keys'), often tinged red and similar to those of the sycamore, are a bonus later in the year.

AUTUMN TINTS

Colourful foliage tints just before leaf-fall are a feature of most acers, but *A. davidii* is not especially vivid in colouring, although the leaves may turn yellow before they fall.

Right: The fruiting 'keys' are an attractive bonus. Starting green, they slowly mature to a pink-suffused red.

Acer griseum

This is a wonderful tree, which always looks interesting, whatever time of year you admire it. It is slow growing so won't readily outstay its welcome. Unfortunately, this same characteristic means that you have to be patient to appreciate its full impact!

A GOOD ALL-ROUNDER

The peeling cinnamon-coloured bark is perhaps the main reason for choosing this tree, but it's a good all-rounder that has other pleasing attractions.

Native to central China, it seems to thrive in cultivation. It's sometimes seen as a multi-stemmed tree or large shrub, but grow it with a clear single trunk for maximum impact as a specimen tree to admire.

PEELING BARK

Sometimes called a paperbark maple, because the outer layer of bark peels off like sheets of brown paper, a mature tree makes an especially eye-catching feature when its trunk is highlighted in winter sunshine.

You may have to wait a few years for maximum effect. The brown bark does not normally start to peel before the wood is three or four years old, then it flakes off to reveal the golden-brown beneath.

FLOWERS AND SEEDS

The pendulous sulphur-yellow flowers in early spring are small but nevertheless a welcome bonus, while the twin-winged 'keys' that help to distribute the seeds in the wind are pleasingly attractive at close-quarters. Don't expect to benefit from these added attractions while the tree is still young.

AUTUMN COLOUR

The summer foliage is olive to grey-green, but towards the end of the season it turns glowing shades of autumnal red and orange. The tree is often seen as its best as low late sunshine brings out the autumn foliage colouring and spotlights the flaking bark below.

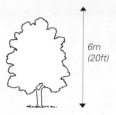

6m
(20ft)

KEY FACTS

SOIL
Undemanding, and will even do well in chalky gardens. Moist but well-drained ground is likely to produce faster growth.

SITE
Best in full sun, but will tolerate light shade.

HARDINESS
Zone 5a

MAINTENANCE
It may be necessary to remove low-growing shoots and branches to ensure a clear trunk is established.

BUYING TIP
You may have to go to a good garden centre or specialist tree nursery ... and expect it to cost more than many commoner trees.

Left: *Acer griseum* is very much a multi-merit tree. Although stunning bark is its main feature, it's an attractive summer tree and super in autumn, when the leaves change colour before they fall.

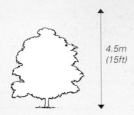

4.5m
(15ft)

Varieties with dissected foliage may be only half this height.

KEY FACTS

SOIL

Prefers a neutral to acid soil, although it will grow on chalky ground provided it is not very dry.

SITE

Best in dappled light or, at least, out of strong midday sun. It will tolerate shade. Avoid a position exposed to strong cold winds.

HARDINESS

Zone 5a

MAINTENANCE

It may be necessary to remove some of the lower shoots as the plant grows, to encourage a more tree-like shape.

BUYING TIP

These trees can resent disturbance, so buy container-grown plants. Choose one with a reasonably straight stem with a tendency to grow upright rather than to branch out.

Acer palmatum f. *atropurpureum*

Surely one of the most beautiful trees for a small garden, this acer never fails to impress with its shapely outline and wonderful colour. And it is just one of many varieties with interesting leaf shapes and colours.

VERSATILE HABIT

You may find this wonderful plant in shrub books as well as those describing trees – it all depends on how it's been trained and whether or not it's a mature specimen. With age, it will make an exceptionally beautiful tree, usually with only a very short trunk, or with multiple stems arising from close to ground level. In leaf it can make a tight mound of foliage that almost obscures the branches and from a distance it can often look like a large shrub.

Unfortunately, it's not the easiest tree to grow if you live in a cold or exposed area, and may require coaxing during the early years. But the rewards are worth it. Spring growth, especially on young trees, may be damaged by cold winds and late spring frosts. New leaves may be killed, but new growth often makes good the early damage. The cut-leaved forms, such as *A.* 'Dissectum Atropurpureum', are particularly vulnerable. Very strong sunshine can also scorch immature leaves.

Grow more than one variety if you have the space and are able to offer suitable conditions, for these beautiful acers will certainly make an eye-catching contribution to your garden.

PURPLE LEAVES

The ordinary species has green leaves that age to bronze or purple towards autumn, but 'Atropurpureum' has deep purple foliage throughout spring and summer. 'Bloodgood' is another especially choice variety, with red new growth that ages to an almost blackish-purple by autumn and followed by the usual firework display of colours before the leaves fall.

There are other varieties in shades of yellow as well as bronze-green and purple, some with leaves more finely dissected.

RED AND SCARLET AUTUMN TINTS

The already colourful foliage becomes even more spectacular before it falls, often creating a flaming display that shouts for attention. The effect can be especially stunning if the tree is planted near a pond where the reflection can double the impact.

Right: *Acer palmatum* 'Dissectum Atropureum' makes a graceful tree, with more finely divided leaves than 'Atropurpureum'.

Amelanchier lamarckii

This tree comes in many guises, sometimes as a large shrub, sometimes as a single-trunked or multi-stemmed tree. And there's even confusion about the name, with one species often masquerading as another. It matters not a jot if you're looking for a good garden plant, for all of them are delightful multi-merit trees that are unlikely to outgrow their welcome in a small garden.

WHAT'S IN A NAME?

These North American and Canadian natives are now naturalized in many parts of Europe, and over the years some have been distributed to gardeners under incorrect names as a result of the confused nomenclature. *Amelanchier lamarckii* is probably the best to choose as a small garden tree, with *A. laevis* a close second. The true *A. canadensis* is a more of a suckering shrub, but in some European countries *A. laevis* may have been distributed under this name.

In any case, they are sure to grace your garden and their varied performance from spring to autumn won't disappoint. Tree forms are sometimes grafted on to a rootstock of hawthorn (*Crataegus laevigata*) or pear (*Pyrus communis*).

The pale grey winter shoots are transformed in mid-spring by the emerging delicate pink to copper-bronze young foliage, and this followed almost immediately by a frothy mass of pure white flowers. These can be fleeting, lasting perhaps a week in warm or windy weather … but then you can enjoy the fresh young leaves as they continue to enlarge and gradually turn green.

SUMMER BERRIES

By late spring and early summer the flowers are just a memory, but in favourable conditions you'll become aware of the ripening berries, turning from red to purple-black as they mature.

AUTUMN FLING

There's a final bid for attention before the leaves drop in autumn, when they often colour wonderfully. *A. laevis* is especially good for autumn colour, with shades of soft red to orange, often with hints of yellow and brown – a showy performance that's often relatively long-lasting.

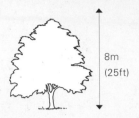

8m
(25ft)

KEY FACTS

SOIL
Undemanding, but thrives best in a well-drained soil that's not too dry.

SITE
Best in full sun but still grows well in partial shade. Does less well in shade.

HARDINESS
Zone 4a

MAINTENANCE
No routine pruning is required, but it may be necessary to remove low branches as the tree grows. Grafted specimens sometimes root poorly and produce suckers, which should be removed.

BUYING TIP
Amelanchiers are widely available, but they will often be shrubby plants with lots of branches from near the base. It may be easier to obtain tree forms, which will have been 'trained', from a specialist grower.

Left: The spring display of white flowers is relatively brief, and the tree may look at its most spectacular for only about a week.

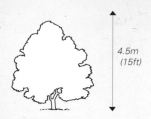

4.5m
(15ft)

KEY FACTS

SOIL
Tolerates most soils, including chalky ground. A soil with a high organic content is likely to produce better growth, however.

SITE
Light shade is ideal, but full sun is tolerated. Although tolerant of coastal regions, avoid cold areas inland.

HARDINESS
Zone 7a

MAINTENANCE
Very biting cold winter winds may damage the foliage, but the tree is likely to grow out of this by the following summer.

BUYING TIP
Always buy container-grown specimens, and expect to have to shop around to find it. You may have to buy from a specialist tree grower.

Arbutus unedo

This is one of the few flowering evergreen trees suitable for a small garden, and if you're patient enough it will make a superb specimen tree that's sure to attract plenty of attention. Unfortunately, it's not a good choice for cold, exposed gardens.

SLOW GROWTH

This slow-growing tree is sometime seen looking more like a large shrub, but in time it will make a choice wide-topped small tree. A native of the Mediterranean region and southwest Ireland, it's relatively cold-tolerant, although a favourable position will ensure a better shaped tree and more rapid growth.

A multi-merit tree, it has late flowers and fruits resembling strawberries – both at the same time!

EVERGREEN LEAVES

Dark, shiny and leathery-looking evergreen leaves, resembling those of a bay tree, make this a good choice where a year-round focal point is required, and is useful where you need something that looks clothed in winter. It's not a particularly useful choice if you want a tree to screen an unattractive outlook, however, as it's too slow-growing to provide quick cover.

PITCHER-SHAPED FLOWERS

The drooping clusters of white or pinkish pitcher-shaped flowers are produced in late autumn and are often still present in early winter. Although they are not large and are inconspicuous from a distance they add interest at a time of year when flowers are especially scarce.

Arbutus unedo f. *rubra* has pinkish-red flowers, but it may not be quite as hardy and vigorous as the white-flowered species.

STRAWBERRY-LIKE FRUIT

The orange-red strawberry-like fruits (perhaps more like cherries with rough, pimply skins) are not often produced in abundance, but they're especially eye-catching. They ripen a year after the flowers are produced, which is why they appear together.

The fruits are edible, although bland, and are used to make a liqueur in some countries.

Right: A mature specimen may carry a conspicuous display of fruits, which make a more prominent display than the flowers from a distance.

Betula pendula 'Youngii'

The graceful and fast-growing birches are popular trees, but most of them quickly grow too tall for a small garden. This weeping form is an elegant tree that's unlikely to become a problem.

GRACEFUL SHAPE

The size, stature and gracefulness of this charming tree makes it instantly appealing, and even a young specimen will soon make an impact. Long after the leaves have fallen the cascade of spreading and weeping shoots makes a pleasing silhouette against the winter sky.

Betula pendula itself, a native of Europe and parts of northern Asia, can grow to 15m (50ft) or more in a surprisingly short time. Young's weeping birch, however, is a form that lacks a dominant leading stem, which means it grows outwards and downwards rather than skywards, so it remains compact. It can be grown on its own stem, but needs careful early training to form an upright trunk, so it's usually grafted as a tall standard, when it makes a small, mushroom-headed tree.

SPRING CATKINS

Although not especially bold, the small catkins can look attractive in early spring when yellow stamens are prominent on the male catkins. Both male and female catkins, which are produced on the same tree, are nearly always formed in autumn, but it's only in spring that they become a conspicuous feature ... a bonus with which to start off the season.

SUMMER GRACE

Summer is the time to appreciate the curtains of pale green leaves that clothe the cascading shoots. To see this pleasing birch at its best, give it an open position where the outline can be viewed against an uncluttered background, ideally with some sky behind. Its charm can be lost if it is planted close to taller trees in the background.

AUTUMN FAREWELL

Although you won't have the fiery farewell produced by some trees that colour well in autumn, this one puts on a more restrained show, with the emphasis on shades of yellow that's nevertheless a delightful farewell gift at the end of another season.

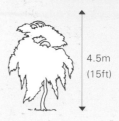

4.5m
(15ft)

KEY FACTS

SOIL
Undemanding, and will grow in almost any soil, but growth may be slow if it's too dry or chalky, and waterlogged soil may cause problems.

SITE
Best in full sun in an open position, perhaps in a lawn, but it will tolerate light shade.

HARDINESS
Zone 1

MAINTENANCE
If growing a tree on its own roots, it may be necessary to tie the young shoot to a vertical support initially until sufficient height has been gained, and to remove some of the lower sideshoots, to produce a suitable trunk.

BUYING TIP
Look for a specimen with a well-shaped head, with branches evenly distributed around it. Make sure there is no weakness or damage near the graft at the top of the trunk.

Left: *Betula pendula* 'Youngii' makes a fine specimen tree set in a lawn, where its shape and cascading branches can be seen to advantage. Its white bark will also become a focal point in winter sunshine.

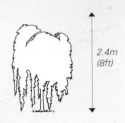

2.4m
(8ft)

KEY FACTS

SOIL
This undemanding plant will grow in almost any soil, including alkaline chalky ground.

SITE
Prefers full sun but will tolerate some shade. Tolerant of cold and exposed positions.

HARDINESS
Zone 2a

MAINTENANCE
If the head looks sparse, hard pruning while the tree is young may stimulate more shoots and a denser head. Watch out for suckers around the base. These will be from the rootstock, and must be removed.

BUYING TIP
The weeping heads are likely to be grafted onto stems 1.5m (5ft) to 2.4m (8ft) high. Although the head may add a little extra height as it fills out, the ultimate height may not be much more than when you buy it. Look for a well-shaped head, with an even cascade of branches all around it.

Caragana arborescens 'Pendula'

This weeping tree is compact enough for the smallest garden – it won't grow to more than about 2.4m (8ft) – and it is really tough, too. It deserves to be grown in small gardens more often.

A PETITE SPECIMEN

Caragana arborescens is an upright, shrubby plant from Siberia and Mongolia that can grow to 4.5m (15ft) or more, but the variety 'Pendula' has cascading growth and is grafted on to an upright stem of the species. This means you can have a small weeping tree that won't outgrow its space.

It's not showy enough to make an impression in a large garden, but in a small one it will make a pleasing display, especially in mid- or late spring when the yellow flowers appear.

Plant it as a specimen tree in a lawn or in the ground, or in a large tub in a patio area. Much of its impact will be lost if you position it among other trees and shrubs in a border.

SPRING FLOWERS

The yellow, pea-type flowers in mid- or late spring resemble those of a broom (*Cytisus*), but they are produced less prolifically. Individual flowers grow on thin, downy stalks, usually as the young foliage is almost fully formed.

SUMMER FOLIAGE

The rather feathery-looking foliage is pale green and pleasing even when the flowers have finished. Other weeping varieties are available with narrower leaves, but the effect is the same from a distance.

To make an impression for the summer months, avoid planting against a backdrop of foliage shrubs, or a hedge, which will lessen the impact.

WINTER OUTLINE

Even in winter this small tree can make a focal point in a small garden if it is suitably positioned. The bare, stiffly pendent branches can look stark yet dramatic when viewed against an appropriate backdrop.

Right: Although the individual flowers of *Caragana arborescens* 'Pendula' are small, the overall display can be quite bold when the plant is in full flower in spring.

Catalpa bignonioides 'Aurea'

Surely one of the finest golden-leaved trees, this is one that stops passers-by in their tracks. The large and bold foliage holds its colour well throughout the summer, and there's the bonus of flowers and interesting seed pods on mature specimens.

VERSATILITY

This beautiful plant is as versatile as it is impressive. It can be grown on a single trunk or as a multi-stemmed tree. Sometimes it resembles a large shrub as much as a tree: it all depends on the early training. It's sometimes even grown as a foliage shrub in a mixed border, being cut back hard each year to stimulate new growth from close to ground level (the resulting shoots often have particularly large leaves). As a specimen garden tree, it's best grown on a single trunk, when it will make a small tree.

  Catalpa bignonioides is native to the eastern United States. 'Aurea' is a little more tender than the green form, as well as being smaller and more compact.

BRIGHT FOLIAGE

The rich yellow leaves do not become dull or turn greenish as the season progresses (a problem with some trees and shrubs with yellow foliage). The leaves have a disagreeable odour when crushed, but this is unlikely to be a problem if you leave them alone, and it certainly should not deter you from planting this excellent tree.

BONUS FLOWERS

In mid- and late summer fairly mature plants produce white flowers with yellowish throats, in long, upright panicles. These are most likely to be produced where the climate is warm or when the summer is a hot one. Although not eye-catching from a distance, they are pleasing and worthwhile for close viewing.

BEAUTIFUL BEANS

If the tree has flowered well, and the summer has been a warm one, you may even have a crop of striking seed pods to admire. These look like large bean pods up to 30cm (1ft) or more long, green at first but ageing to black. They become a feature in early autumn, and will usually remain hanging into winter, long after the leaves have fallen.

Left: In time *Catalpa bignonioides* 'Aurea' can make a substantial tree, but it will take years to reach this size.

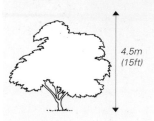

4.5m (15ft)

KEY FACTS

SOIL
Best in fertile soil, and is unlikely to do well in shallow or impoverished soil.

SITE
A sheltered position is better than an exposed one, otherwise the large leaves maybe damaged. It's likely to do best in a warm and sheltered position. Partial shade may ensure the yellow leaves do not scorch, but they do grow well in full sun.

HARDINESS
Zone 5a

MAINTENANCE
If you want a tree with a single clear trunk, remove low-growing branches while it is young if necessary.

BUYING TIP
If you want a single-stemmed tree, be sure to get one that is suitably trained and with a single dominant leading shoot, rather than a shrubby plant that has several stems near the base.

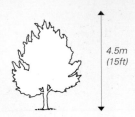

4.5m
(15ft)

KEY FACTS

SOIL
Requires well-drained soil to
do well. Although best on
neutral or acid soil, good
specimens can still be grown
on chalky soil if it's not too
thin. It's unlikely to do well
on heavy clay.

SITE
Full sun or light shade. It
looks best in a lawn or open
situation.

HARDINESS
Zone 6a

MAINTENANCE
Little needed.

BUYING TIP
You may not find a specimen
with a long, clear stem. This
plant is more often grown as
a multi-stemmed tree. At
first it may look shrub-like,
but several main trunks will
develop from close to the
base and form a spreading
tree. Container-grown plants
are likely to grow away more
readily than rootballed ones.

Cercis siliquastrum

Cercis siliquastrum has all the qualities needed to
make an interesting feature in a small garden. It is
almost smothered with bright rose-purple flowers in
late spring and early summer, remains small for many
years and usually develops an interesting spreading
shape that gives old specimens a special appeal. The
common name of Judas tree alludes to the legend
that it was on one of these trees that Judas hanged
himself after the betrayal of Christ.

SLOW GROWTH
This pretty native of the eastern Mediterranean region is a sun-
loving tree that does best in warm areas. It's not a good choice for
a cold or exposed position. One of its quirky features is the ability
to produce flowers directly from the trunk, or an old branch, as well
as the young branches where you'd expect to find them.

It's a good choice where a specimen tree in a lawn is required.
Plant with the future in mind: this is a relatively slow-growing tree,
sometimes more like a large shrub, which has spreading growth
that could be a problem if you put it too close to other trees or
shrubs. In a lawn, or given plenty of space, it will be relatively
attractive while young, yet still look magnificent and uncramped
when it becomes a mature tree.

MASSES OF FLOWERS
The pea-type flowers are usually rose-purple, but there are varieties
with deep purple flowers, and even a white one.

These appear in late spring at about the same time as the new
leaves. If the foliage is not well developed at this time, the flowers
can give the impression of a rosy-purple mist from a distance.

INTERESTING PODS
Flattish seed pods, 8–10cm (3–4in) long, start to be conspicuous
from midsummer. Grey-green at first, they age to a greyish-brown,
sometimes with a purplish tinge, and persist into winter.

AUTUMNAL COLOUR
Although autumn tints are not as spectacular as the fiery reds and
oranges of some trees, the dying leaves put on a pleasing display
in shades of yellow.

Right: *Cercis siliquastrum* is often seen as a multi-stemmed tree, and while
young can look like a large shrub. You can also train it as a more upright tree
with a single main trunk.

Cornus kousa

This attractive multi-merit tree has all the qualities you could require: a spectacular display of flowers, fascinating fruits and superb autumn colour. Moreover, it is unlikely to become so large that it outgrows its space. Consider this choice tree if you want something special and have the patience to wait for your rewards.

SLOW GROWTH

You will often find this described as a shrub, but given 20 or so years it will become a charming small tree with a bushy habit. Its slow growth means you'll have to wait to see this, but the plus side is that it makes a delightful shrubby plant for a small garden while young. This choice tree is a native of Japan, Korea and central China, and it possesses that special quality that suggests a sense of Oriental beauty. It deserves to be planted more widely, particularly if you can provide conditions in which it will grow quickly and thrive.

SHEETS OF BRACTS

What might appear to be flowers from a distance are in fact large white bracts (modified leaves): the true flowers are small and inconspicuous in the centre of each set of four bracts. They are borne freely in late spring and early summer, when the spreading branches appear laden with them.

The botanical variety *C. k.* var. *chinensis* is an especially fine form, usually flowering even more prolifically and with larger bracts. It's likely to flower in early summer, the bracts beginning green and maturing to pure white.

STRAWBERRY FRUITS

In a favourable year strawberry-like fruits may be produced, though not often in anything like the profusion of the flowers. These are edible, but both seedy and insipid in taste.

FIERY FINAL FLING

In some gardens the autumn leaf colours can be dramatic, in rich shades of bronze and crimson. As with all autumn colour, the effect is better in some years than in others. The autumn colour may start early, and linger longer than on most trees ... sometimes for as much as a month before the leaves fall.

Left: *Cornus kousa* flowers prolifically, though the 'petals' are actually bracts. This specimen is multi-stemmed, but the tree is often seen grown with a single trunk.

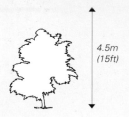

4.5m
(15ft)

KEY FACTS

SOIL
This is a demanding tree, requiring a deeply cultivated acid or neutral soil to do well. Performance on shallow or chalky soils is usually disappointing.

SITE
Best in light shade, but will grow in full sun. Avoid heavy shade.

HARDINESS
Zone 5a

MAINTENANCE
Little required.

BUYING TIP
You're most likely to find this plant at a specialist tree nursery.

Cotoneaster 'Hybridus Pendulus'

If your garden's really minute or you're looking for a feature for a patio, try this tiny tree. It is really a prostrate shrub grafted on top of a straight stem, so you can be sure it won't grow much taller than when you buy it.

WEEPING HABIT

Don't expect a large tree-like plan – it will be more the size of a tall standard rose, though on a mature plant the branches will be more spreading. It's really a prostrate ground-cover shrub, which when grafted to the top of a tall stem of a suitable rootstock, such as *C. bullatus*, forms a weeping standard. Although it is often recommended for a very small garden, it makes a splendid feature plant for a large garden too, perhaps set in a lawn.

The main attraction are the bright red berries with which the stems are festooned in autumn, though the small white flowers are an added interest in early summer.

This semi-evergreen hybrid of garden origin probably has *C. dammeri* as one parent and *C. frigidus* as the other, though *C. salicifolius* may have been involved.

SHOWERS OF FLOWERS

Individually, the small white flowers are uninspiring, but they are produced in profusion, the drooping stems being studded with them in early summer.

BERRY-STUDDED STEMS

Brilliant sealing-wax-red berries are produced in such profusion in autumn that the trailing stems appear to be weighed down by them. Even better, they normally persist well into winter.

The slightly glossy leaves, about 8cm (3in) long, help to set off the red berries, forming an ideal backdrop.

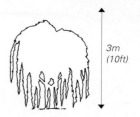

3m
(10ft)

KEY FACTS

SOIL
Undemanding and will grow well on most soils, though growth may be slow and poor on very shallow chalky ground.

SITE
Tolerates sun or shade, but best in full sun. Avoid dense shade.

HARDINESS
Zone 5a
(less if grafted on a shorter stem)

MAINTENANCE
Little routine maintenance required.

BUYING TIP
The height at which the head has been grafted onto the main stem can vary between about 1.8m (6ft) and 3m (10ft), so look for one that's about the height you want. If ordering from a nursery remember to specify that you want a tree (standard) form.

Left: This cotoneaster forms a small, weeping tree when grown as a standard. There are small white flowers in summer and red berries in autumn.

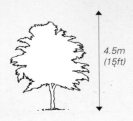

4.5m
(15ft)

KEY FACTS

SOIL
These undemanding plants will grow in any soil.

SITE
Best in full sun, but happy in partial shade.

HARDINESS
Zone 5a

MAINTENANCE
Suckers sometimes appear from the rootstock around the tree. These should be removed as soon as they are noticed.

BUYING TIP
As these varieties are budded or grafted, make sure that the site of the bud or graft appears strong and undamaged. Look for a neat, symmetrical head.

Crataegus laevigata 'Paul's Scarlet'

Don't ignore this small, compact tree just because it is undemanding and easy to grow. These are qualities enough to justify a place on any shortlist, but its neat growth and masses of red double flowers make it one of the finest small trees for late spring colour.

A GOOD SPECIMEN TREE

This double-flowered red 'thorn' originated in 1858 as a mutation on a double pink variety, and it has to be one of the best crataegus for flowers.

You may find it listed as a variety of C. oxyacantha (it's been a victim of name-changing by botanists), and synonyms for the varietal name are 'Coccinea Plena' and 'Kermesiana Plena'. The species itself is native to Europe, including Britain.

Try this tree as a specimen in a lawn: the head is carried well above the ground, the leaves are small and the growth compact enough not to cast too much shade. You'll also find this an easy tree to mow up to and around.

FLOWER POWER

The species itself has small, white, single flowers, but 'Paul's Scarlet' is a much more striking tree, with double, pinkish-red flowers freely produced in late spring and early summer. 'Rosea Flore Pleno' is similar but pink, while 'Plena' is a white double that ages to pink. All are well worth growing.

BERRY BONUS

Most crataegus produce plenty of red berries in autumn, but unfortunately you pay a price for the more impressive flowers on these double varieties. Berries may be produced, but they will be scant. If you're looking for autumn interest, consider one of the other crataegus, such as C. persimilis 'Prunifolia', which is described on page 75.

Right: Crategus laevigata 'Paul's Scarlet' is one of the finest hawthorns to grow for a floral display. It makes a small, neat-looking tree, and although individual flowers are small the overall effect can be stunning.

Crataegus persimilis 'Prunifolia'

If autumn interest is more important than spring flowers, this is one of the best crataegus to consider. Both berries and autumn foliage tints are impressive, and when you have both together the combination is impressive.

A THORNY ISSUE

Although it is probably a North American native, the origins of this tree are a little clouded. It may be a hybrid of *C. crus-galli*. You may find it labelled *C. prunifolia*. Provided you look for the word 'prunifolia', you will be planting an outstanding small tree.

It will form a rounded head of branches, sometimes wider than high, and often with branches quite close to the ground. This may make it difficult to mow beneath if planted in a lawn, but it makes a good focal point plant in a grassed area.

The fiercely thorned branches are densely clothed with glossy green leaves, dark above and pale beneath, attractive all summer but superb when they colour in autumn.

WHITE FLOWERS

The clusters of white flowers in early summer are not the main reason for growing this tree, though they are a useful bonus. If you want brighter or more impressive flowers, at the expense of a good autumn display, consider the varieties of *Crataegus laevigata* described on page 72.

BEAUTIFUL BERRIES

In autumn the bunches of rich red berries are a prominent feature for many weeks. At first they are set off against the green leaves, then these turn into a glowing crimson and the red berries and autumn foliage colour combine to create a superb spectacle.

FLAMING LEAVES

In autumn the leaves flare into a blaze of orange and crimson, enhanced by the red berries that make a happy combination.

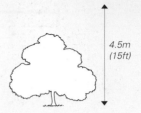

4.5m
(15ft)

KEY FACTS

SOIL
These undemanding plants will grow in any soil.

SITE
Best in full sun, but happy in partial shade.

HARDINESS
Zone 5a

MAINTENANCE
Can be slow to establish, but should eventually grow more rapidly. If you don't want low-growing branches making mowing the grass a potentially prickly hazard, remove some of them to give a greater length of clear trunk.

BUYING TIP
Check that the area of the budding or grafting is firm and healthy and does not look weak. Choose a tree with evenly balanced growth.

Left: *Crataegus persimil 'Prunifolia'* looks best in autumn, when it's usually laden with red berries. Autumn foliage colour is good too, and for a while you may be able to enjoy both at once.

Eucryphia x nymansensis 'Nymansay'

There aren't many trees that flower in late summer and early autumn, but this choice plant is one of them and it is evergreen into the bargain. It can be a demanding plant to establish, but is well worth the effort if you can provide suitable conditions.

AN UNCOMMON TREE

You may find this hybrid between two South American species, and some other eucryphias, described and listed as shrubs, but those such as *Eucryphia* x *nymansensis* can make much-branched columnar trees. They are not particularly common as trees, so your eucryphia will probably look rather special.

'Nymansay' is quite fast-growing, which is a further attraction. Unfortunately, it needs a mild and favourable area to do well.

WHITE FLOWERS

The white flowers with yellow stamens resemble Christmas roses (*Helleborus niger*) and look especially good against the backdrop of dark, glossy, evergreen foliage. Usually, the tree is covered with them from top to bottom, making it attractive whether viewed close to or from a distance.

Individual flowers may be 5cm (2in) or more across.

EVERGREEN FOLIAGE

This is one of a small and select group of trees with large, showy flowers that's also evergreen. This particular tree is a hybrid between two Chilean species, *E. cordifolia* and *E. glutinosa*, and it can be variable, having both compound and simple leaves on the same plant.

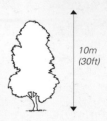

10m
(30ft)

KEY FACTS

SOIL
Thrives best on acid or neutral, moisture-retentive but not waterlogged soil. Alkaline, chalky soils sometimes produce acceptable results, but only if deeply cultivated.

SITE
Light or partial shade is preferable to a very sunny position. The roots must be in shade, even if the top is in full sun. Avoid a position prone to strong winds.

HARDINESS
Zone 7a

MAINTENANCE
It may be necessary to remove dead or winter-damaged shoots in mid-spring. New growth is usually produced to replace it provided you do not live in an especially cold area.

BUYING TIP
Buy a container-grown specimen, and plant it during spring rather than autumn. You will probably have to buy this tree from a specialist tree grower.

Left: *Eucryphia* x *nymansensis* 'Nymansay' can make a beautiful upright tree in time and is a magnificent sight even from a distance.

Fagus sylvatica 'Purpurea Pendula'

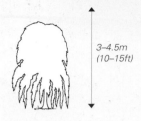

3–4.5m
(10–15ft)

Anyone who knows how what large and majestic trees the purple beech can be, may have doubts about planting one in a small garden! But this weeping form can be planted with confidence, as it makes a distinctive, small, mushroom-shaped bush.

SPACE-SAVER

Whether you find this tree attractive or unappealing is a matter of individual taste. It is not a graceful tree, like *Betula pendula* 'Youngii' (page 61), but a rather tight mushroom shape with somewhat angular growth. This means it's very space-saving and compact, and ideal if you want a purple-foliaged tree suitable for a small space.

Use it as a patio or lawn specimen rather than in a mixed border, or among other trees, or its impact will be lost. The dark leaves show up best against a light background such as a lawn.

You may find conflicting advice regarding the eventual height of this tree. Some experts suggest that, although slow-growing and remaining small for many years, it will eventually grow large. It may be that there are different forms of the tree, but don't let this doter you – it is unlikely to outgrow its welcome in the timespan most of us plan for.

PURPLE LEAVES

The purple-red spring foliage ages to dark bronze-purple, but always makes a strong impact. The tightly packed pendulous shoots mean the leaves form a tight purple curtain around the tree, often to ground level.

MUSHROOM SHAPE

While young the mushroom shape is very attractive, but old specimens tend to become more flat-topped. The weeping growth makes sure that it is a distinctive tree in summer, and the outline of the bare branches can make an interesting winter feature.

KEY FACTS

SOIL
Generally undemanding, but avoid heavy clay soil.

SITE
Full sun, ideally in a lawn where its colouring and shape can be appreciated.

HARDINESS
Zone 5a

MAINTENANCE
If the head seems to be developing unevenly, prune out a few shoots while the tree is still young to create a more balanced shape.

BUYING TIP
You will usually need to go to a specialist nursery to obtain this tree.
Look for a specimen with branches that are well-spaced around the head.

Left: As the leaves fall in winter, the pendulous outline of the branches still adds interest by creating a structured shape that can be a focal point when set in a lawn.

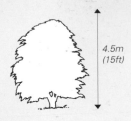

4.5m
(15ft)

KEY FACTS

SOIL
Undemanding and does well on most soils, but best on fertile, moisture-retentive but well-drained ground.

SITE
Tolerates sun or shade, but for a well-shaped tree a sunny position is needed to ensure even growth and an attractive shape

HARDINESS
Zone 6a

MAINTENANCE
If the formative training has not been complete, it may be necessary to shorten long sideshoots at the top by about half to stimulate more branching.
If you want a longer trunk, as the tree grows remove some of the lowest shoots. Variegated varieties may produce all-green shoots, which should be cut out as soon as they are noticed.

BUYING TIP
You may have to go to a specialist tree nursery to find a holly trained as a standard or tree form. Hollies do not transplant well, so they should be bought as container grown specimens.

Ilex aquifolium

The ever-popular holly is usually seen as a large shrub, but you can also enjoy it as a fairly large pyramidal tree or a small tree with a clear trunk. They can be clipped to shape when they look especially impressive in a formal setting.

STANDARD FORM

The best form to consider as a small garden tree is one trained as a standard, with a rounded head at the top of a clear stem. These look especially pleasing in a formal setting, or even in large containers.

Pruning will easily keep your tree within bounds once the head has grown to a size that you find appropriate.

MALE OR FEMALE?

Unfortunately male and female flowers are often carried on different plants (though some are bisexual). If you have a variety that has all-male flowers you won't get berries. And even if you buy a female variety, you'll need a male plant somewhere nearby to obtain a good crop of berries.

You can't judge sex by the name. 'Golden King' is a female, while 'Golden Queen' is male! Check with your supplier.

EVERGREEN LEAVES

The species itself has green evergreen foliage, but most of the varieties grown in gardens are chosen for their variegated leaves. There are lots of them, with gold or silver the most common.

Typically the leaves are spiny, but some varieties, such as *Ilex aquifolium* 'J.C. van Tol', have almost spineless foliage.

BRIGHT BERRIES

Not all varieties produce berries, so make sure you choose an appropriate one, and have a pollinator.

Typically, the long-lasting berries (often still present in spring after a mild winter if the birds haven't been driven to strip them from the tree) are bright red. But even that's not always so, as 'Amber' and 'Bacciflava' ('Fructu Luteo') are among those with yellow berries.

Right: *Ilex aquifolium* 'J.C. van Tol' is a good choice if prickly leaves deter you from growing holly.

Juniperus scopulorum 'Skyrocket'

Choose this distinctive conifer if you want to create tall points and a vertical dimension without taking up too much space. It is an ideal tree whenever you want maximum impact in minimum space. If you are looking for a narrow columnar conifer, this is one of the very best. The name 'Skyrocket' indicates its apparent desire to reach skywards rather than explore horizontally.

ACCENT ON HEIGHT

It's a splendid accent plant to punctuate a bed that needs a little height, but a single specimen in a lawn or a fairly flat area can look a little out of place. In that situation it's best to plant a small group of them (at least three, and possibly five or more in larger areas).

You may sometimes find this distinctive conifer sold or listed as a variety of *Juniperus virginiana*. There has been debate amongst botanists over its origins (it was found in the wild as a seedling), but whichever of these North American species it's derived from, you can be sure it's a good choice for a small garden.

BLUE-GREY FOLIAGE

At close quarters the foliage is seen to be made up of small, sharp-pointed scale-like leaves, with awl-shaped juvenile foliage. The overall impression from a distance is of a blue-grey tree.

PENCIL-LIKE SHAPE

The narrow columnar habit that gave this conifer its name is what makes it such a useful garden tree.

It's quite a rapid grower, and makes a statement within a few years of planting. Growth slows with age, but even a tall specimen probably won't look out of place because of its small 'footprint'.

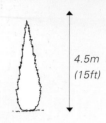

4.5m
(15ft)

KEY FACTS

SOIL
Undemanding, and tolerates chalky and dry soils well.

SITE
Best in an open, sunny position.

HARDINESS
Zone 3a

MAINTENANCE
Little required.

BUYING TIP
If buying a number of plants to form a group (often an effective way to grow these narrow trees), choose plants that are well-matched in size and shape.

Right: *Juniperus scopulorum* 'Skyrocket' can be used as a single specimen focal point as it has been here, but in a large garden a group of three or five often looks better.

Laburnum x watereri 'Vossii'

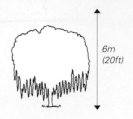

6m
(20ft)

Don't dismiss the laburnum just because it's a commonly planted tree. The reason so many gardeners choose it reflects its qualities as a good garden tree: quick growth coupled with a small ultimate size and a showy display of bright and cheerful flowers.

SPRING SPECTACULAR

The widely planted laburnum needs little introduction, as it's such a bright and spectacular sight in late spring and early summer, when its branches are festooned with long, drooping chains of yellow flowers.

The only negative thing about the laburnum is its reputation for being poisonous. Although it is a poisonous plant, the only significant danger is if children eat the seeds, which are contained within pea-like pods. 'Vossii' is usually chosen because it produces fewer seeds than most other kinds, but it's also a superior plant anyway with extra-long racemes of flowers, which can reach up to 60cm (2ft).

Laburnum x *watereri* itself is a hybrid between *L. alpinum* and *L. anagyroides*, which though still available are not so widely planted as the hybrids.

GOLDEN CHAINS

A common name sometimes used is golden chain tree, a reference to the long, drooping, tassel-like racemes that are covered with yellow pea-type flowers in late spring or early summer. The flowers open at about the same time as the leaves, which means that they are not obscured by the foliage.

The flowers are lightly scented, although not everyone realizes this because you have to be very close to the blooms to appreciate the fragrance.

SUMMER APPEARANCE

When seed pods are produced they hang all summer, long after the seeds have been shed. The branches have upright growth initially, but can become spreading with age. The grey-green trifoliate leaves give the tree a rather dull appearance once the flush of new growth is over, but this is a price worth paying for such a spectacular floral display earlier in the year.

Left: Golden chain and golden rain tree are names often used for laburnums, and are particularly appropriate for *L.* x *w.* 'Vossii'

KEY FACTS

SOIL
Undemanding, and even grows well on chalky soils.

SITE
Best in full sun, but will tolerate light shade.

HARDINESS
Zone 6a

MAINTENANCE
On small trees the mature, brown seed pods, which are not particularly attractive, can be cut off.
To keep a single-stemmed tree in shape, simply trim off the higher sideshoots as necessary.
Laburnums respond well to pruning and training, and can be used to form arches or tunnels.

BUYING TIP
You'll have no problem finding this popular tree – it's stocked by most outlets. If you want a specimen with a single tall trunk, make sure it has a long and clear main stem with an undamaged leading shoot.

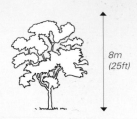

8m
(25ft)

KEY FACTS

SOIL
Best on a fertile, loamy soil, and does very well on clay. Not ideal for chalky soils.

SITE
Light shade is well tolerated. The tree itself will do well in sun, but avoid planting it where early morning sun will fall on the flowers.

HARDINESS
Zone 5a

MAINTENANCE
If you don't want a wide-spreading shrubby tree, remove some of the lower branches in the dormant season.
If it doesn't show signs of flowering after five years, root pruning may help to induce flowering.

BUYING TIP
This magnolia is only rarely sold as a pre-trained standard tree with clear trunk. If you're prepared to settle for a spreading multi-stemmed tree, choose one with balanced growth all around the plant, and an undamaged leading shoot.

Magnolia x soulangeana

Justifiably one of the most widely planted magnolias, this magnificent tree is a real show-stopper in spring when the bare branches are laden with huge and beautiful blooms. Provided it can be given space to spread, this surely has to be on any shortlist.

SPRINGTIME ELEGANCE

This hybrid raised in the garden of Soulange-Bodin, at Fromont near Paris, is surely one of the most popular of all flowering trees. It's a hybrid of *M. denudata* fertilized by the pollen of *M. liliiflora* (both Chinese species). It makes a multi-stemmed, spreading tree, and it's the spread as much as height that might limit where you plant it in a small garden. A mature tree can be 10m (30ft) across, though it will take many years to reach this size.

Apart from the spelling used above, you are likely to encounter this tree spelled *soulangiana*. The difference simply reflects changing rules of nomenclature.

In some ways magnolias are more like large shrubs, and their spreading habit makes them more suitable as a lawn tree rather than cramped in a border.

Many varieties have been raised, varying mainly in flower size and colour, though some varieties flower a little later or earlier than others. The normal flowering time is mid-spring, before the leaves emerge, but cultivars like 'Lennei' may not bloom until late spring. Overfeeding them will lessen or even prevent flowering.

The flowers do not mind light frost, but will go brown if they thaw rapidly in direct sunlight.

BEAUTIFUL BLOOMS

The crowning glory of this magnificent tree is undoubtedly the profusion of large flowers resembling white tulips and stained rose-purple at the base.

Particularly impressive varieties include 'Lennei' (flowers like enormous creamy-white goblets suffused rose-purple), 'Lennei Alba' (ivory white) and 'Rustica Rubra' (pinkish, cup-shaped flowers).

Some varieties are pleasantly scented, but flower size, shape and colour are usually considered the more important qualities.

AUTUMN LEAVES, WINTER BUDS

There's another brief flush of colour in autumn as the leaves turn yellow. Before winter's out the developing flower buds become conspicuous.

Right: *Magnolia x soulangeana* 'Amabilis' has ivory-white flowers with just a hint of a purple flush at the base of the inner petals.

Malus floribunda

A delightful tree when covered with blossom in spring, this ornamental crab apple has all the qualities needed for an exceptionally good small garden tree. And it's just one of many outstanding trees in the genus that you could use.

RELIABILITY

This Japanese tree – some experts consider it to be a hybrid rather than a true wild species – is perhaps the most beautiful of all crab apples when in blossom. The branches are garlanded with flowers in spring, making an outstandingly beautiful sight.

It's a round-headed tree, sometimes spreading with age, and an utterly reliable choice. It's undemanding to grow, flowers while still young, grows reasonably quickly, yet is unlikely to outgrow its space.

BEAUTIFUL BLOSSOM

This willing tree blossoms in mid- to late spring, the whole tree almost smothered with flowers. Although individual blooms are not large, the overall impact is impressive.

The flowers are rich rose when half-open, but fade to pale pink when fully expanded, creating an overall impression of a pale blush when viewed from a distance.

SMALL FRUITS

This is not the best choice if you're looking for a *Malus* with a heavy crop of conspicuous crab apples. The round, pale yellow fruit are relatively small, at about 18mm (¾in) across.

PURPLE AND RED

Malus x *purpurea* is similar to *M. floribunda*, but has purplish-red leaves, and red flowers. Its coloured foliage makes it a more attractive tree during the summer months.

If you want a green-leaved crab apple with red flowers, try *M.* x *atrosanguinea*, which is very like *M. floribunda* but a richer rose, which does not fade as the flowers mature.

There are also many hybrid crab apples with attractive blossom and fruits, so it's worth looking at other varieties too.

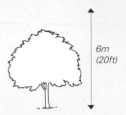

6m
(20ft)

KEY FACTS

SOIL
Undemanding, provided the soil does not become waterlogged.

SITE
Will tolerate light shade, but best in full sun.

HARDINESS
Zone 4a

MAINTENANCE
Unlike ordinary apple trees, *Malus floribunda* does not require routine pruning.

BUYING TIP
Look for an attractive and balanced head, and make sure there are no signs of pests or disease.

Left: *Malus floribunda* is grown mainly for its spring blossom, but you may have a few crab apples in autumn as a bonus. There are better *Malus* for autumn fruits, however.

Malus 'John Downie'

Wonderful in spring with its blossom, and spectacular in autumn when laden with colourful fruit, this is justifiably one of the most popular ornamental crab apples. This hybrid has been in cultivation for more than 100 years. By general consent, it is one of the very finest crab apples for fruiting. Not only does it crop prolifically, but the fruit is among the largest and most colourful of all. Being large the fruit is also popular for making crab apple jelly.

SPRING FLOWERS

The blossom appears in late spring, pink in bud opening to white. The tree is perhaps not as pretty as *M. floribunda* (page 89), but still very attractive when in full bloom.

COLOURFUL FRUIT

The main reason for growing 'John Downie' is undoubtedly its crab apples: large in comparison with other varieties, rather conical in shape, and a wonderful combination of yellow changing to bright orange and red.

There are other hybrids that hold their fruit for much longer (such as *Malus* x *zumi* 'Golden Hornet'), but 'John Downie' is so showy that one can forgive its more transient display. The fruits don't hang very long before beginning to drop. They can make a mess if they overhang a path, and the fallen fruit is best raked up from a lawn. But rather than waste them, pick them just before they fall to make crab apple jelly.

If you shop around you'll find many other *Malus* with colourful fruit that are a feature of autumn and even continue into winter. Some of the outstanding varieties to look for are 'Golden Hornet' (yellow), *M.* x *schiedeckeri* 'Red Jade' (long-lasting red fruits on weeping branches), and two cultivars of *M.* x *robusta*: 'Red Sentinel' (deep red fruits that hang well into winter) and 'Red Siberian' (red fruits prolifically produced).

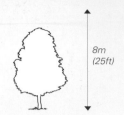

8m
(25ft)

KEY FACTS

SOIL
Undemanding, provided the soil does not become waterlogged.

SITE
Full sun, best seen as a lawn specimen.

HARDINESS
Zone 6a

MAINTENANCE
Unlike ordinary apple trees, crab apples do not require routine pruning, though it's worth pruning occasionally to maintain an open centre to the tree. This will encourage the fruits to ripen and colour well.

BUYING TIP
Buy a tree about 2–3m (6–10ft) high, with evenly distributed branches forming a balanced head.

Left: *Malus* 'John Downie' is also a very pleasing blossom tree, the white flowers making a useful contribution to the garden in late spring.

Malus tschonoskii

This tree is a wonderful choice where you need a crab apple with narrow, upright growth, and it is one of the very best for fiery autumn colours.

This native of Japan can grow tall by the standards of many of the trees included in this book, but its erect, rather columnar growth means it doesn't take up much ground space.

It lacks the flower-power of most crab apples, and the fruit isn't especially noteworthy (brownish-yellow flushed purple, and only sparsely produced), but is nevertheless a tree worth growing for its shape and often brilliant autumn colour.

SPRING FLOWERS

The late spring white flowers, about 2.5cm (1in) across, are flushed pink at first. Although the blossom is not as freely produced as on say *M. floribunda* (page 89), it's nevertheless a showy tree in flower.

AUTUMN COLOUR

Autumn is when this tree excels over most other *Malus*, and its moment of glory is shortly before the leaves fall. The foliage assumes shades of yellow, orange, purple and scarlet, all the more conspicuous if the tree is fairly tall and standing in a spot where its profile and colour can be appreciated, perhaps as a specimen tree in a lawn.

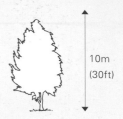

10m
(30ft)

K E Y   F A C T S

SOIL
Undemanding, provided the soil does not become waterlogged.

SITE
Full sun, best seen as a lawn specimen.

HARDINESS
Zone 6a

MAINTENANCE
Unlike ordinary apple trees it does not require routine pruning. Stem canker can be troublesome and usually requires the removal of the affected branch.

BUYING TIP
Sometimes available at good garden centres; otherwise buy from a specialist tree nursery.

Left: Although *Malus tschonoskii* has pretty spring flowers and small fruits in autumn, it's really at its best when the foliage turns.

Prunus 'Amanogawa'

One of the best Japanese cherries for a small garden, this tree is wonderful in flower, with attractive autumn colour and a narrow columnar growth habit that means it doesn't take up much space.

JAPANESE BEAUTY

This is one of the many Japanese cherries, evolved in the gardens of that country over two or three centuries, that make excellent small garden trees. It's now difficult to be sure of the species from which they derived, but it matters not a jot in gardening terms: we must just be thankful that they're there.

You might see it described as a variety of *Prunus serrulata*, as this is the species from which most of the Japanese cherries are thought to be descended, but it's more often sold simply as *P.* 'Amanogawa'.

Don't expect cherries too! It does sometimes produce a few small black fruits, but they are insignificant and of no merit.

This Japanese cherry is grafted or budded on to a rootstock from another prunus (such as *P. avium*), close to the ground so that a tree with branches almost from the base is formed.

SEMI-DOUBLE FLOWERS

The pretty shell pink flowers in mid- to late spring have about nine petals, making them semi-double, though some may be single. They're also fragrant, though you need to be close to the tree to appreciate their delicate scent.

AUTUMN FAREWELL

In spring the young leaves are greenish-bronze, becoming green in summer, then before they fall bidding a bold farewell. Typically, the leaves turn shades of orange, yellow and flame, though like the autumn display of most trees the performance varies from year to year.

COLUMNAR GROWTH

Japanese cherries are noted for their beautiful blossom, but this tree is especially distinctive because of its fastigiate (narrow and pillar-like) growth, rather like a Lombardy poplar, although, of course, it is a much smaller tree.

Even in winter, when the leaves have fallen, the column of upright-growing bare branches can look distinctive and surprisingly attractive against a bright sky.

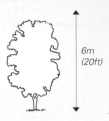

6m
(20ft)

KEY FACTS

SOIL
Undemanding, and will do well on chalky soil. Avoid ground prone to waterlogging.

SITE
Full sun.

HARDINESS
Zone 7a

MAINTENANCE
Remove any suckers by pulling them away rather than cutting them off, which should reduce the risk of regrowth.
Where heavy snowfalls are common it may be worth tying strong string around the branches in several places to reduce the risk of them bending under the weight of snow.

BUYING TIP
Look for a specimen well clothed with branches along most of the length of the stem. It's normal for this tree to be 'feathered' to the base rather than have a clear trunk.

Left: The narrow, upright growth of *P.* 'Amanogawa' makes it a particularly useful tree where you want a vertical element without too much spread.

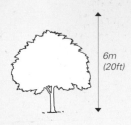

6m
(20ft)

KEY FACTS

SOIL
Undemanding and will grow well on most soils, but it's best to avoid very impoverished and dry soils.

SITE
Best in full sun. Will tolerate light shade, but the leaf colour will be affected by heavy shade.

HARDINESS
Zone 4a

MAINTENANCE
The length of the trunk can be increased over the years by removing more of the lower sideshoots as they grow.

BUYING TIP
If you want a tree on a clear trunk, make sure the young specimen you buy is already well formed, rather than shrubby-looking.

Prunus cerasifera 'Pissardii'

This is one of the most effective of the purple trees, seen in many small gardens. You can plant it secure in the knowledge that, although it grows rapidly when young, it is unlikely to outgrow its welcome.

IMPACT

Prunus cerasifera is a shrubby tree native to western Asia and some other areas, but it's the purple-leaved varieties that are popular garden trees. *P. c.* 'Pissardii' (sometimes seen simply as *P. pissardii*) is one of several with dark foliage that are easily confused from a distance. You may sometimes see it listed as 'Atropurpurea'.

'Pissardii', discovered before 1880 by M. Pissard, gardener to the Shah of Persia, has dark purple leaves. The similar 'Nigra', a selection from 'Pissardii', has darker blackish-purple foliage and darker flowers.

The growth is bushy, and the plant can be grown as a hedge, as it will withstand the necessary trimming. As a tree it forms a rounded head, sometimes on a short trunk.

Careful positioning is necessary to get the best from these trees, as the dark foliage means impact is lost if planted with a tall dark hedge, or other trees, in the background. Choose a fairly open position where the tree can be appreciated.

SPRING FLOWERS

One of the earliest trees to flower, in early spring, this has buds that start pink but open to white. They're usually plentifully produced, and open before the leaves, or at about the same time; this early blooming means the flowers are all the more welcome.

The flowers in the similar 'Nigra' open pink, then fade to blush.

COLOURFUL LEAVES

Young foliage is dark red, but it ages to deep purple. 'Nigra' has blackish-purple mature foliage.

OCCASIONAL FRUITS

This form of plum tree does produce fruits, but not reliably and they are often few in number. They are dark purple to almost black, round and quite small.

Right: *Prunus cerasifera* 'Pissardii', a useful tree for a small garden though it's best positioned against a light background so that the purple foliage can be seen to advantage.

Prunus 'Kanzan'

A particularly popular Japanese cherry, for many this spectacular tree epitomizes the whole group. Laden with spring blossom, and almost brash with its large double pink flowers, it's sure to make a statement in your garden.

SPECIMEN TREES

Another hybrid raised in Japan many years ago, this has all the classic form of a Japanese cherry. 'Kanzan' (which may be spelt 'Kwanzan' in the USA) is a rendering of the ideogram for a Chinese mountain sacred to Buddhists, which gives some indication of its pedigree.

In flower, it's a real eye-catcher, with its rather stiffly ascending branches richly wreathed in blossom. But these features can make it look out of place in an informal or cottage-style garden.

It makes a good 'avenue' tree, planted in two long rows that you can walk between, but a single specimen can also look superb if carefully placed. Initially the branches are held in an upright, vase shape, but as the tree matures they open out to form a spreading crown. A single specimen is perhaps best used in isolation in a lawn. Its quite large size and distinctive shape generally make it unsuitable for planting in a border.

SPRING BLOSSOM

The branches are smothered with large, double, dark pink flowers, hanging in bunches, in mid- or late spring. These open purplish-pink but turn paler pink later.

AUTUMN FLING

Although the tree is uninspiring in summer, it puts on another bold display in autumn, when it goes out with a colourful display of autumn colour, the leaves turning bronzy-orange before they fall. The dark green leaves are edged with fine teeth and end in a slender, tapering point.

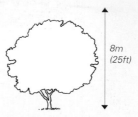

8m (25ft)

KEY FACTS

SOIL
Undemanding, but it's best to avoid impoverished or very dry soils.

SITE
Tolerates light shade, but best in full sun.

HARDINESS
Zone 5a

MAINTENANCE
This tree is prone to diseases such as silverleaf, and to reduce the risk of infection should not be pruned unless really necessary.

BUYING TIP
Look for a well-shaped head and check that there is no sign of damage to the trunk or branches. Large trees do not transplant well, so don't be put off by a small specimen.

Left: *Prunus* 'Kanzan' is a magnificent flowering cherry that makes a good specimen tree in a lawn. It is almost brash in bloom, but few flowering trees pack as much punch in full flower.

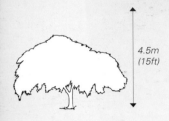

4.5m
(15ft)

KEY FACTS

SOIL
Tolerates most soils, but it's
best to avoid poor,
impoverished ground.

SITE
Full sun.

HARDINESS
Zone 7a

MAINTENANCE
If suckers appear from the
rootstock, remove them
promptly, pulling them off at
source if possible.

BUYING TIP
Look for a well-shaped tree
with undamaged weeping
branches well distributed
around the crown.

Prunus 'Kiku-shidare-zakura'

This is a good choice if you want a Japanese cherry
but don't have much space – its weeping growth
ensures a bright and bold display on a small tree that
won't take up a lot of room.

BEST WEEPING CHERRY

Perhaps the best weeping cherry for a small garden, this small tree
has arching branches, which droop gracefully to the ground. They
are studded with pretty double, pink flowers in spring, followed
by bronze-green young leaves that later become a glossy green.

Although it is sometimes used as a patio tree, it's probably best
planted in a lawn. The cascading pink flowers look superb against
the green grass, and the tips of the long cascading branches are
less likely to be damaged by contact with a lawn than a hard
surface such as paving.

It's worth clarifying the nomenclature, which can be confusing.
You may sometimes see this tree labelled 'Cheal's Weeping'
cherry', which is an invalid (but widely used) name. As with many
Japanese cherries, you will also find variations with hyphenation
and spellings. You'll sometimes find it without the hyphens, or as
'Kiku-shidare Sakure'.

FLOWERING CURTAINS

The clear pink flowers hang like curtains on stems that can reach
to the ground, a superb sight in mid-spring. They are so packed
with petals that they resemble small chrysanthemums.

Right: *Prunus* 'Kiku-shidare-zakura' is an ideal weeping cherry for a small
garden if it can be grown in the centre of the lawn. Its tumbling branches are
laden with pretty pink blossom in spring.

Prunus sargentii

Here's an outstanding tree that will give you a blossom display in spring and an autumn show that's just as magnificent. It's one of the finest of all trees for autumn colour.

A LITTLE LARGE?

Although not such a popular tree for small gardens as most of the other *Prunus* described in this book, this is nevertheless considered by many to be the loveliest of all flowering cherries. It can be quite large, and only just qualifies for entry in this book on height grounds. While not suitable for a really small garden, it's a good choice where you have a little more space. It is quick-growing initially, then slows down and becomes a fairly flat-topped tree.

In the wild, and in very good conditions in gardens, it can easily exceed the height given here, but not for many years, and in most gardens it will probably remain a tree of modest size. But give it space to develop if possible, so that it makes a well-shaped tree.

This native of Japan, Korea, and the Sakhalin peninsula is reliable and easy to grow, and deserves wider planting in gardens wherever there's space for it.

SPRING BEAUTY

Individual flowers are small and single, but borne in such profusion on the bare branches in early or mid-spring that the overall impression packs plenty of punch. The bright pink flowers are often joined by coppery-red emerging leaves, a wonderful combination.

The cultivar 'Rancho' flowers a little earlier and has slightly larger flowers and a narrower growth habit.

The flowers sometimes lead later to small, black, cherry-type fruits, but these are not an important feature of the tree.

AUTUMN COLOUR

This is one of the first trees to turn colour, usually in early autumn. It also gives a reliable performance, unlike the quality of autumn colour of some trees, which can depend very much on the season. Dominant colours include orange and crimson.

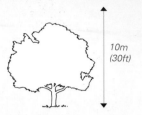

10m
(30ft)

KEY FACTS

SOIL
Undemanding but may not perform well on very poor and impoverished soil.

SITE
Will tolerate shade, but is best in sun.

HARDINESS
Zone 4a

MAINTENANCE
Little required.

BUYING TIPS
You may have to buy this plant from a specialist tree nursery. Look for a tree with a well balanced head (those tend to be bushy, branching trees, and a long clear trunk may not be necessary). Bare-root trees transplant during the dormant period but at other times buy container-grown specimens must be used at other times.

Left: Although *Prunus sargentii* may eventually grow too large for a very small garden, this will take many years.

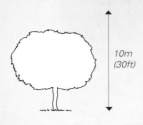

10m
(30ft)

KEY FACTS

SOIL
Undemanding, and will grow
well on most soils.

SITE
Full sun or light shade, but
for maximum visual impact
choose a position that
receives lots of winter
sunshine.

HARDINESS
Zone 5

MAINTENANCE
Remove lower branches as
the tree grows to produce a
longer trunk.

BUYING TIP
You're likely to have to buy
this tree from a specialist
tree nursery. Look for a
straight, undamaged trunk.

Prunus serrula

This tree is well worth growing for its bark alone. It looks so appealing that you'll simply want to keep touching it. It's likely to be a star attraction during the winter months.

SPECIMEN TREE

Native to China, this distinctive tree is grown primarily for its beautiful bark. It's a small but vigorous tree with narrow, willow-like leaves and small white flowers in mid-spring. There are much more impressive *Prunus* species to grow for showy flowers, but the outstanding bark is something you'll enjoy for the whole year, not for just a week or two.

It makes a pleasing 'avenue' tree, planted in rows that you can walk between, but few small gardens have space for this. The best position in most gardens is as an isolated specimen in a lawn, preferably where its bark can be highlighted by winter sunshine.

SMALL FLOWERS

The small, single flowers, which open towards the end of mid-spring, are white. They are usually produced in clusters of twos and threes at the same time as the new foliage, which means they are sometimes rather concealed by the leaves.

Small, round, cherry-like black fruit is sometimes produced but is not a feature.

BEAUTIFUL BARK

Bark may sound boring, but you simply can't pass by this tree without admiring its beautiful trunk. The surface of new bark looks like glistening, polished, reddish-brown mahogany. Older bark peels, like that of some maples and birches, to reveal the highly polished new bark beneath. A number of other *Prunus* species have interesting barks. Among them are *P. maackii*, which has yellowish-brown bark, and *P. x schmittii*, which has purplish-red bark, horizontally banded in orange-brown.

Right: *Prunus serrula* is a tactile as well as a visual tree. It is difficult to resist touching the trunk as you walk past it, and its lovely bark looks wonderful in winter sunshine.

Prunus x *subhirtella* 'Autumnalis'

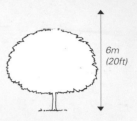

6m
(20ft)

Trees that flower in winter have to be worth considering. The flowers may be small, but their very presence will cheer you up when all around seems grey and miserable.

This is a tree that comes into its own in the dreary months between late autumn and spring. That's when the small flowers begin to open, often while the autumn foliage is still colourful, and whenever the weather's not too cold and severe you're likely to find a few of them right through until spring.

WINTER CHEER
It's another wonderful tree from Japan, well worth trying to include on your shopping list of highly desirable trees. Be sure to plant it near a path that you use regularly in winter or where you can see it easily from a window on those cold, dull days.

AUTUMN COLOUR
The leaves usually turn a rich red and bronze before they fall in autumn.

WINTER FLOWERS
The small, semi-double, white flowers, pale pink in bud, are not particularly bold individually, but clustered along the bare branches they make a very welcome sight from late autumn onwards. You will usually find at least a few flowers out through until early spring, but they'll be at their most prolific during the milder weather of late autumn and early spring. Flowering will be affected by very cold weather. Sometimes, however, if blooming has been inhibited by cold weather during the winter, these trees will compensate by giving an extra special display in spring.

Try cutting a few shoots for indoor winter decoration, when you'll really appreciate fresh flowers from the garden.

'Autumnalis Rosea' has pink flowers, while those of 'Fukubana' are a rich, warm pinkish-red.

KEY FACTS

SOIL
Will tolerate most soils well, but avoid poor and impoverished soil or ground prone to waterlogging.

SITE
Will grow well in full sun or light shade, but is seen best in a sunny position ideally with a dark background such as a hedge behind to show off the pale flowers to advantage.

HARDINESS
Zone 5a

MAINTENANCE
Trim off the lower shoots as the tree grows to keep the trunk clear.

BUYING TIP
Choose your tree carefully, as some are trained as bushy plants to make a small shrubby tree. If you want a clear trunk choose one that is already growing that way.

Left: *Prunus* x *subhirtella* 'Autumnalis' has good autumn colour and pretty flowers from late autumn to early spring.

Pyrus salicifolia 'Pendula'

One of the best foliage trees for a small garden, this relative of the pear is an outstanding weeping specimen that looks wonderful in a lawn.

It's difficult to appreciate that this is a kind of pear until you look closely in autumn and spot the typical pear-shaped fruits. Its leaves are more willow-like, and its weeping habit means that it makes a tumbling mound of growth that trails to the ground.

TOUGH TREE

The species, a native of southeast Europe, Asia Minor and the Caucasus, is a tough tree that seems to look right in most gardens, large or small. Although in time it will grow to the height suggested here, and maybe even a little larger in ideal conditions, it will remain a small tree long enough for most of us not to mind planting it in a garden of modest size.

Although usually planted as a specimen tree in a lawn, it makes a pleasing feature planted towards the back of a shrub or mixed border.

WHITE FLOWERS

The creamy-white flowers, about 18mm (¾in) across, open in mid-spring, set in calyces and flower stalks covered with white 'wool'. They usually open simultaneously with the leaves, which appear silvery white for the first few weeks, creating a very pleasing picture.

SILVERY LEAVES

Although the narrow, willow-like, leaves open a silvery-white colour, they become grey-green. The overall effect when the long, pendulous branches are densely covered with foliage is of a silvery-grey mound.

DISTINCTIVE FRUIT

The fruits, 2.5–5cm (1–2in) long, are hard and of no culinary value. Visually, they are an interesting bonus to appreciate at close quarters but are barely noticeable from a distance.

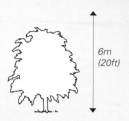

6m
(20ft)

KEY FACTS

SOIL
Undemanding, but is unlikely to do well on poor, impoverished ground.

SITE
Full sun.

HARDINESS
Zone 4a

POSSIBLE PROBLEMS
Largely trouble free.

BUYING TIP
Choose a specimen with an evenly balanced head and branches spaced fairly regularly around the crown.

Left: *Pyrus salicifolia* 'Pendula' is one of those trees that seems to look right in any garden, whatever the size. It makes a mound of silvery foliage.

Rhus typhina

You're as likely to find *Rhus typhina* described and sold as a large shrub as you are a tree, but whether you grow it as a shrubby, multi-stemmed tree or on a single stem with a typical tree-shaped head, it will make a statement as a focal point.

FLAMBOYANCE

This is primarily a foliage tree, grown for its large pinnate leaves, at their most wonderful as they assume their autumnal colours. Once the leaves have fallen it looks gaunt yet dramatic in its own distinctive way.

Native to eastern North America, this tree can make a spectacular lawn specimen. Unfortunately, suckers are a recurring problem so some gardeners prefer a site where these are easier to remove, such as in a border. They will root so can be given to friends!

Most *Rhus* are known as sumach (or sumac). Common names for *R. typhina* include staghorn sumach, velvet sumach and Virginia sumach.

SUMMER FOLIAGE

The leaves often reach 60cm (2ft) and are divided into pairs of leaflets along their length (pinnate leaves). They are covered with brownish hairs while young, but become smooth by autumn, though the stalks remain downy. *R. typhina* 'Dissecta' (more widely sold and grown in gardens as 'Laciniata') is a striking female form with deeply cut leaflets that create a more fern-like impression.

AUTUMN COLOUR

In autumn these large and magnificent leaves turn yellow, red and orange and the whole tree becomes a blaze of colour.

FLOWERS AND FRUIT

Male and female flowers are borne on different plants in late summer. The female flowers form dense pyramids 10–20cm (4–8in) long. The fruits are also packed closely together in dense upright bristly cones, covered with crimson hairs, which turn brown and are retained into winter. The male flowers form large green clusters, and lack the appeal of the female form.

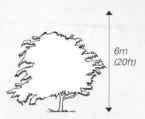

6m (20ft)

KEY FACTS

SOIL
Any reasonable garden soil.

SITE
Will grow in light shade but does best in full sun.

HARDINESS
Zone 3a

MAINTENANCE
Remove suckers by excavating the soil around them and pulling them off rather than cutting, if possible. Wear stout gloves, as the plant can cause allergic reactions.

BUYING TIP
You may have to buy *R. t.* 'Dissecta' from a specialist tree nursery. Check with the supplier that it is the female form. If you want a tree grown as a standard rather than a multi-stemmed form, look for one that has been trained with a clear stem.

Left: *Rhus typhina* is grown primarily for its large foliage, which shows fabulous autumn colour, but its curious flower heads are a useful bonus. The fruits form bristly cones, which turn brown and are retained into winter.

Robinia pseudoacacia 'Frisia'

Though possibly on the large side for some gardens, you often see this tree planted even in tiny plots, such is the attraction of the golden leaves. Where space is limited, it's surprising how well it can adapt in both size and shape and still look good.

VERSATILITY

The species is native to the eastern United States, but this cultivar was raised in a Dutch nursery in about 1935. It's now recognized as one of the very finest golden-leaved deciduous trees that can be grown. Its appeal lies not only in its golden colour, but also in the graceful growth habit and sprays of feathery pinnate leaves.

Although it makes a pleasing specimen tree in a lawn, it's an exceptionally good tree to plant towards the back of a shrub or mixed border, or against a dark backdrop, where the bright foliage will shout its presence. It's also possible to create some wonderful colour combinations, such as planting one of the forms of purple-leaved *Cotinus coggygria* in front of it.

If you want a smaller robinia, try *R. p.* 'Umbraculifera', which is sometimes distributed as 'Inermis'. It's a small, mop-headed tree with a distinctive shape.

GOLDEN TREASURE

Many trees and shrubs with yellow leaves lose their brightness as the season progresses and become greener, but 'Frisia' retains its bright golden-yellow through until autumn.

OTHER ATTRACTIONS

The thorns on young growth are red, though this is not a feature you're likely to notice on an established tree because they will usually be above eye level. Mature trees produce racemes of white pea-type flowers in early or mid-summer, sometimes in abundance, though these are not so conspicuous against the yellow foliage as the green of the species. They are unlikely to be found on young specimens.

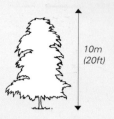

10m (20ft)

KEY FACTS

SOIL
Performs best on moist (but not waterlogged), fertile ground, and may do poorly on very alkaline (chalky) soil.

SITE
Best in full sun, and will tolerate light shade. Avoid heavy shade as this will produce greener leaves.

HARDINESS
Zone 3a

MAINTENANCE
Little required.

BUYING TIP
Widely available, usually as a standard tree with a clear stem. However, it can also be grown as a shrubby specimen so make sure you choose one suitably trained if you want a traditional tree with a single trunk.

Above left: Although grown primarily for its golden foliage, a mature tree will have a deeply grooved bark that has its own special appeal.

Left: The pinnate leaves of *Robinia pseudoacacia* 'Frisia' always seem to look bright and fresh. Although they do darken in colour towards the autumn, they remain light and bright for most of the summer.

Salix caprea 'Kilmarnock'

Being exceptionally small, this weeping tree is one that you're sure to be able to find space for. It's at its prettiest in spring, but the weeping shape and small stature make it a pleasing plant all year round.

This charming small weeper is also likely to be found under its synonym, *Salix caprea* 'Pendula'.

MALE AND FEMALE

Salix caprea itself is a shrub or small and bushy tree, native to northwest Asia and Europe, including Britain. It's best known for the very silky catkins produced on bare stems in early spring. The male catkins are the showiest, about 2.5cm (1in) long or a little more; the female catkins grow to almost 5cm (2in), but are not as silky and showy. Nevertheless, they are a popular spring feature.

'Kilmarnock' is a male, though a very similar female form called 'Weeping Sally' (*S. caprea* var. *pendula*) is sometimes available.

SILVERY CATKINS

The catkins are silvery when they emerge, due to the silky hairs, but look yellow when they are fully expanded and open. The period from emerging silvery buds to fully open catkins lasts several weeks and can last from early to mid-spring, by which time the leaves are emerging.

WEEPING SHAPE

The weeping branches are stiffly pendulous. The outline is quite attractive in winter, but especially pretty when the branches are studded with emerging catkins. When the leaves have fully expanded the foliage forms a delightful green umbrella.

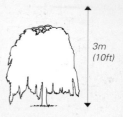

3m
(10ft)

KEY FACTS

SOIL
Requires fertile, moisture retentive soil to do well, and is unlikely to thrive on infertile or shallow soils.

SITE
Full sun.

HARDINESS
Zone 5a

MAINTENANCE
Little required.

BUYING TIP
Choose a specimen with a nicely balanced head with the pendulous shoots reasonably evenly spaced all around. If you're really bothered about the kind of catkins it may be worth checking with your supplier (or going to a specialist tree nursery).

Left: There's surely room in almost every garden for a dwarf weeping tree like *Salix caprea* 'Kilmarnock'. It is at its most attractive in spring, when the catkins are out. The foliage follows a little later.

Sorbus vilmorinii

Sorbus are popular for their feathery foliage and bright berries in late summer and autumn, and if you're looking for one suitable for a small garden, this is one to try. It's a graceful tree with many merits, and more compact than most species.

RESTRAINED ELEGANCE

This beautiful tree from western China has a restrained elegance, which makes it a tasteful rather than brash choice. Its feathery-looking foliage and graceful habit are especially appealing, and it has the advantage of not being as tall as many of the *Sorbus* that are grown for their berries and autumn colour.

It makes a bushy tree or a more upright plant with a typical standard head. Some experts consider that there are two forms in commercial production.

This is a tree to grow among a collection of other trees, provided it is not crowded out, or as an isolated specimen in a lawn.

There are many other superb *Sorbus* with attractive and long-lasting berries, and it is worth considering some of these if you have space for a tree that may grow taller than *S. vilmorinii*.

FERNY FOLIAGE

The foliage, which is almost fern-like as it opens, is composed of pinnate leaves with lots of small leaflets along their length. During the summer it's a rather dull green, but nevertheless unoppressive and feathery-looking on graceful branches.

AUTUMN COLOUR

In autumn the leaves become tinted with purple and red, a worthwhile display on its own but even more attractive when studded with the colouring berries as well.

CHAMELEON BERRIES

Individual berries are small but held in large and showy, loose drooping clusters. They gradually change colour from a glossy red at first, fading through pink to white with a pink flush.

Not only can you enjoy the gradual transitions from one colour to another, you will also be able to benefit from berries that persist for longer than those of many other *Sorbus* species. They usually remain hanging decoratively on the naked branches long after the foliage has fallen.

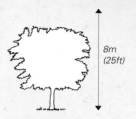

8m
(25ft)

KEY FACTS

SOIL
Undemanding and will do well on most soils.

SITE
Full sun. Will tolerate light shade, but the foliage and berry colour may not look so good in autumn.

HARDINESS
Zone 6a

MAINTENANCE
Little required.

BUYING TIP
You will probably have to buy *S. vilmorinii* and *S. hupehensis* var. *obtusa* from a specialist tree nursery, but *S.* 'Joseph Rock' is a popular cultivar, which is more readily available.

Left: 'Joseph Rock' is a wonderful rowan. It has yellow berries and good autumn colour. When these appear at the same time the result can be stunning. It's also an undemanding, easy-to-grow tree.

Ulmus glabra 'Camperdownii'

As this small weeping tree is commonly planted in parks, its familiarity may blind you to its merits as a tree for small gardens. But if you are looking for a small weeping tree to plant in a lawn, this might be just what you need.

A MINIATURE ELM

Ulmus glabra itself is a large tree that makes an imposing feature in the landscape of its native Europe and northern and western Asia. Don't be put off though, because a lot lies in a name, and if you see 'Camperdownii' added to it you'll know that it's going to make a small tree that you can confidently plant in your front garden, even if it's tiny. You might sometimes see it sold or described simply as *Ulmus* 'Camperdownii'. It arose as a seedling at Camperdown House in Dundee, Scotland.

It makes a distinctive focal point as a specimen tree in a lawn, needing to be planted in an open position, in reasonable isolation, for its shape and form to be appreciated.

MUSHROOM HEAD

The appeal of this weeping tree lies in its mushroom-like shape. The tree is usually top-grafted (grafted at the top of a tall rootstock), and the stems tumble sharply to ground level to produce a mushroom-shaped dome. While it makes an intriguing tree in summer when cloaked in a cloth of green, the bare stems make an attractive feature in winter.

GREEN CURTAIN

The drooping stems are usually clothed to the ground with green foliage, as though draped with a green tablecloth. The colour is light to mid-green, becoming darker as the season progresses. It ends in a flash of yellow before the leaves fall in autumn.

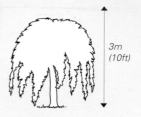

3m
(10ft)

KEY FACTS

SOIL
Undemanding and will grow in almost any soil.

SITE
Best in full sun but will tolerate light shade.

HARDINESS
Zone 5a

MAINTENANCE
In countries where Dutch elm disease (a fatal fungal disease spread by a bark beetle) is prevalent, check regularly for any dieback.

BUYING TIP
In areas where Dutch elm disease is prevalent, you may be able to obtain this tree only from specialist tree nurseries.

Look for an evenly balanced head with branches well distributed all around.

Left: *Ulmus glabra* 'Camperdownii' makes a green dome in the summer, but the tumbling branches are a feature even in winter. This spring shot gives you a good idea of its multi-season attributes.

Ulmus minor 'Dampieri Aurea'

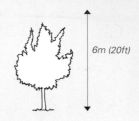

6m (20ft)

A rather narrow, columnar profile and bright golden foliage make this a distinctive tree that once encountered is seldom forgotten. It imprints itself on your memory once you've been captured by its special beauty.

ORIGINS

Botanically this distinctive tree is of doubtful origin, and over the years it has been renamed a number of times, but there's no doubt about its garden merit. It's upright shape and golden colour make a striking punctuation point in the garden, especially if it's planted among darker trees or towards the back of a shrub border. You may find it under a range of names, which include *Ulmus* x *hollandica* 'Dampieri Aurea', *U*. 'Dampieri Aurea', *U*. x *hollandica* 'Wredei', *U*. 'Wredei' and even *U*. 'Wredei Aurea'. Given time, botanists may yet reclassify it again! Don't be deterred by this chequered background, for it's a distinctive tree, well worth considering except for a very small garden.

This was once considered to show tolerance to Dutch elm disease. Unfortunately, it will succumb, so in areas subject to this disease it's a potential problem to bear in mind. However, you may well consider it a risk worth taking for such a striking garden tree.

GOLDEN ATTRIBUTES

This is a tree grown primarily for its foliage colour, as its tiny pale green flowers in early spring are uninteresting and will probably go unnoticed. The leaves, however, are distinctive and conspicuous: coarse-textured on both surfaces, golden-yellow (a colour retained throughout the summer) and crowded close together.

UPRIGHT GROWTH

Forming a tight, upright pillar, this is a distinctive tree that looks like a column of gold in summer and has structural value in winter.

KEY FACTS

SOIL
Undemanding and should grow in any soil.

SITE
Full sun or light shade.

HARDINESS
Zone 5a

MAINTENANCE
In countries where Dutch elm disease is prevalent, check regularly for any dieback.

BUYING TIP
You may find this relatively difficult to obtain in areas where Dutch elm disease has made the various species of *Ulmus* an unpopular choice. It is, however, available from specialist tree nurseries.

Left: *Ulmus minor* 'Dampieri Aurea' combines a narrow, columnar habit of growth with bright golden foliage, features that make it ideal as a focal point tree for a small garden.

small trees at a glance

	EVERGREEN	DECIDUOUS	HEIGHT	SOIL TYPE				
				CHALK	DRY	MOIST	ACID	ALKALINE
Abies koreana	•		8–9m (25–30ft)	•		•	•	
Acer davidii		•	8m (25ft)	•		•		•
Acer griseum		•	6m (20ft)	•		•		•
Acer palmatum f. atropurpureum		•	4.5m (15ft)	•		•		•
Amelanchier lamarckii		•	8m (25ft)			•	•	
Arbutus unedo	•		4.5m (15ft)	•				•
Betula pendula 'Youngii'		•	4.5m (15ft)	•		•	•	
Caragana arborescens 'Pendula'		•	2.4m (8ft)		•			
Catalpa bignonioides 'Aurea'		•	4.5m (15ft)	•		•		
Cercis siliquastrum		•	4.5m (15ft)			•		
Cornus kousa		•	4.5m (15ft)	•		•		
Cotoneaster 'Hybridus Pendulus'	•		3m (10ft)	•	•			
Crataegus laevigata 'Paul's Scarlet'		•	4.5m (15ft)	•	•	•	•	•
Crataegus persimilis 'Prunifolia'		•	4.5m (15ft)	•				
Eucryphia x nymansensis 'Nymansay'		•	10m (30ft)			•	•	
Fagus sylvatica 'Purpurea Pendula'		•	3–4.5m (10–15ft)	•				•
Ilex aquifolium	•		4.5m (15ft)	•		•		
Juniperus scopulorum 'Skyrocket'	•		4.5m (15ft)	•	•			
Laburnum x watereri 'Vossii'		•	6m (20ft)				•	
Magnolia x soulangeana		•	4.5m (15ft)			•		
Malus floribunda		•	6m (20ft)	•		•		•
Malus 'John Downie'		•	8m (25ft)	•		•		•
Malus tschonoskii		•	10m (30ft)	•		•		•
Prunus 'Amonogawa'		•	6m (20ft)	•		•		•
Prunus cerasifera 'Pissardii'		•	4.5m (15ft)	•		•		•
Prunus 'Kanzan'		•	8m (25ft)	•		•		•
Prunus 'Kiku-shidare-zakura'		•	4.5m (15ft)	•		•		•
Prunus sargentii		•	10m (30ft)	•		•		•
Prunus serrula		•	10m (30ft)	•		•		•
Prunus x subhirtella 'Autumnalis'		•	8m (25ft)	•		•		•
Pyrus salicifolia 'Pendula'		•	6m (20ft)	•				•
Rhus typhina		•	6m (20ft)	•		•		
Robinia pseudoacacia 'Frisia'		•	6m (20ft)	•	•			
Salix caprea 'Kilmarnock'		•	3m (10ft)			•		
Sorbus vilmorinii		•	8m (25ft)	•				•
Ulmus glabra 'Camperdownii'		•	3m (10ft)			•		
Ulmus minor 'Dampieri Aurea'		•	6m (20ft)			•		

| | SITUATION | | | HABIT | | | | FOLIAGE | | | FEATURES | | |
SHADE	COASTAL	PROTECTED	UPRIGHT	SPREAD	WEEPING	COLUMNAR	VARIEGATED	GOLD	GREY	AUTUMN	BARK	FLOWERS	FRUIT
			•						•				•
•			•			•				•	•		•
•										•	•	•	•
•				•						•		•	•
•				•								•	•
	•	•		•									
•					•					•			
					•							•	
		•		•				•				•	•
•				•					•				•
•						•				•	•		•
•					•								
•				•								•	
•			•									•	•
•						•							•
•					•					•			
•			•				•						•
						•			•				
												•	
•		•		•								•	
				•						•		•	
			•							•		•	
			•							•		•	
			•									•	
			•									•	•
			•									•	
					•							•	
				•						•		•	•
				•						•		•	•
				•						•		•	•
					•				•			•	•
			•							•			•
						•		•					
					•							•	
•				•								•	•
•					•								
•			•					•					

INDEX

Page numbers in *italic* refer to the illustrations

ACKNOWLEDGEMENTS

Executive Editor: **Emily van Eesteren**
Editorial Manager: **Jane Birch**
Executive Art Editor: **Peter Burt**
Designers: **Anthony Cohen, Jane Coney**
Picture Researcher: **Charlotte Deane**
Production Manager: **Louise Hall**

Photography

A–Z Botanical Collection/Derek Ditchburn 112/P. Etchells 39/Mike Vardy 74

Eric Crichton 12 bottom

Garden Picture Library/David Askham 26/Brian Carter 22 bottom/David England 62/Vaughan Fleming 101/John Glover 88/Marijke Heuff 118/Michael Howes 38/Jerry Pavia 68/Ros Wickham 40 right

John Glover 10 top, 10 bottom, 11, 19 top, 19 bottom, 20 top, 22 top, 24–25, 44, 59, 60, 76

Harpur Garden Library 45, 110

Andrew Lawson 9, 13, 18, 23, 28, 40 left, 56, 90, 106, 116, 120

S & O Mathews 8, 12 top, 16, 20 bottom, 41, 55, 67, 87, 98, 108

Peter McHoy 84, 105, 114

Octopus Publishing Group Limited 48/Sean Myers 2–3, 4–5, 6–7, 14–15, 29, 30 top left, 30 top right, 30 bottom, 31 top, 31 bottom, 32 top, 32 bottom, 33 top left, 33 bottom left, 33 right, 35, 36–37, 46–47, 51, 52, 64, 70, 81, 97, 122–123

Photos Horticultural 27, 78

Harry Smith Collection 73, 92, 94, 102

Tree-shape artworks

Trevor Lawrence